# Real-Life Case Studies for School Administrators

William Hayes

## The Scarecrow Press, Inc.
### Technomic Books
### Lanham, Maryland, and London
### 2000

SCARECROW PRESS, INC.

Published in the United States of America
by Scarecrow Press, Inc.
4720 Boston Way, Lanham, Maryland 20706
www.scarecrowpress.com

4 Pleydell Gardens, Folkstone
Kent CT20 2DN, England

British Cataloguing in Publication Information Available

**Library of Congress Cataloguing-in-Publication Data**

Hayes, William, 1938–
    Real-life case studies for school administrators / William Hayes
        p.    cm.
    ISBN 0-8108-3742-0 (paper : alk. paper)
    1. School administrators—United States—Case studies. 2. School
management and organization—United States—Case studies. I. Title.
    LB2806.H39    2000
    371.2'00973—dc21                                    99-053068

Printed in the United States of America

♾$^{TM}$ The paper used in this publication meets the minimum requirements of American
National Standard for Information Sciences—Permanence of Paper for Printed Library
Materials, ANSI/NISO Z.39.48–1992.
Manufactured in the United States of America.

# CONTENTS

# Preface

Successful school administrators have to be people with vision and the ability to lead others. They also have to be able to manage conflict and crisis. Because of our nation's increasing diversity and divisiveness, these skills are perhaps now more important than ever. Superintendents, principals and other administrators face a staggering array of educational, political and ethical problems and must frequently deal with several of these dilemmas at the same time.

I have heard it said that school administrative courses do not effectively prepare students to deal with the "real life" problems they will face in their jobs, so the case studies in this book deal with authentic situations faced by administrators. Each one of them is based upon an actual situation. In determining the types of cases to be included, I have sought to introduce problems relating to the kinds of knowledge and skills administrators must possess. For me, this information is best described in the book *Principals for Our Changing Schools: The Knowledge and Skills Base.* This book, edited by Scott D. Thomson, was produced by the National Policy Board for Educational Administration, an umbrella group that contains representatives of all of the professional organizations concerned with the education of school administrators. It was published by Technomic in 1993 and provides a wealth of information on research in the field, as well as performance standards for school administrators. I believe that the knowledge and skills outlined in *Principals for Our Changing Schools* can be enhanced and augmented when students work with their professors to react to the cases included in this book.

In addition, the issues raised in this book can be great assistance in preparing administrators for future certification examinations, which are being considered in many states. Based on the national standard/skills proposed for administrators, these tests will emphasize problem-solving. Along with the input of a knowledgeable instructor, discussion of the case studies contained in this book might be the best possible preparation for the examinations that educational administration students will be facing. The book is organized so instructors can quickly evaluate which cases will best supplement the study of any specific aspect of an administrator's work. The table of contents includes the themes of each case. All of the cases include a brief introduction, which outlines the problem to be considered. Reading the introductions will tell instructors enough about the case to determine if it is appropriate for the objectives of the class. At the end of each case is a series of possible discussion questions, which can provide the basis for initiating a classroom conversation on the case.

This case-study book can supplement a primary text in any administration course. Perhaps most useful in a survey class, it can also be very effective in any course dealing with personnel or policy development. Because the book includes cases on almost every phase of educational administration, students could be required to purchase it when entering an administrative program, and various cases could be used in each course offering. For instance, several cases would be appropriate in a class on educational finance, and a number could be used in a general management course.

I have found that any topic being studied can be enhanced by having students engage in a discussion of realistic problems. The cases can be assigned as an outside reading assignment, with the students being asked to respond to the possible discussion questions at the end of each chapter. At times the instructor might want to add additional questions. The cases can also be assigned to a group of students. This is especially helpful when a problem requires technical or legal research. Groups can be given sufficient time to find the appropriate background information and then be asked to make a formal presentation to the class. Students or groups can also be encouraged to seek solutions from practicing administrators.

I believe that experienced teachers and administrators will recognize the realistic nature of the situations described in these cases and that each case will provide the basis for spirited group problem-solving. It is my hope that the dialogue stimulated by this book will provide valuable learning experiences and enliven classroom discussions. Since there are no simple answers to the questions raised by these cases, they should help students to better understand the ambiguities and difficulties that face administrators on a daily basis.

# Acknowledgments

I would like to acknowledge the valuable assistance of several individuals in helping to prepare this publication. A special thanks is in order to Janine Wingerter, who made valuable suggestions for several portions of the manuscript. Kristen Bianchi, a student secretary in the Teacher Education Division of Roberts Wesleyan College, not only typed the entire book but greatly enhanced the text with her many editorial suggestions. This project was made possible by Kristen's outstanding work. Finally, I would thank my wife, Nancy, for her patience, careful proofreading, and insightful recommendations.

*Case Study 1*

# The Person in the Middle

When contract negotiations between the school district and faculty union are going poorly, the building principal can become the person in the middle. Although the principal is theoretically part of the management team of the district, others often make negotiation decisions. At the same time, the principal must work on a daily basis with faculty members who are unhappy and sometimes angry. Despite these conditions, the building principal must attempt to ensure that the school continues to function with a minimum of disruptions. This can be extremely difficult, as the principal cannot help but have strong feelings about school crises.

As Bob Lewis was opening his car door to leave for home, he noticed a large number of cars across the athletic field in the elementary school parking lot. For a moment, he could not think of the reason for the crowd, but then remembered the local teacher's union was having a meeting. Contract negotiations had been going on for over a year and both the union and the Board of Education were stubbornly maintaining their positions on salary increases and health insurance benefits. The current impasse had been going on for months and tension levels were high. Relations between the teachers and the board had become strained, with charges and countercharges being aired.

As the high school principal, Bob Lewis could feel the tension when he entered the faculty room of his school. Teachers talking about the problem would quickly become silent when they saw him. He had never experienced this kind of reaction during his eleven years as principal. As a former social studies teacher in the district, Bob had developed a friendly but professional relationship with the school's teachers. During negotiations, he had always maintained a neutral position and avoided conversations with anyone except the members of the administrative management team. Although there had been some discussion of the talks at administrative meetings, decisions on the district positions and strategy in the talks were being made by Superintendent Ron Clark and a three-member board of education personnel committee. The three committee members were part of a

1

conservative majority on the board who believed that teachers were overpaid and underworked. The superintendent was young and new to the district and there was little question that he was increasingly seen by many on the faculty as merely a puppet of the board's conservative majority.

Not being part of the management negotiations committee, Bob felt helpless in regard to the contract talks. At the same time, he didn't feel that he could talk about negotiations with his old friends on the faculty, because of his position as a member of management. Tom Bianchi was the union president and an old friend, but they had never discussed the issues. They came to the school district together almost twenty years ago and had become very close, but lately Tom was preoccupied and their relationship seemed to be changing.

As he drove the five miles to his home, Bob thought about several negotiation problems that he had to deal with in the coming week. The teachers in each building were gathering in the parking lot before school for meetings. During these early morning sessions, the officers and the negotiating team would update the teachers on the progress of negotiations. Following the meeting, the teachers would solemnly walk into the building in pairs. This had not been a problem, but this morning they had come in several minutes late. The corridors were filled with students waiting to get into their homerooms and for several minutes Bob was the only one in the high school with over one thousand teenagers. Had there been an incident, there is little doubt that the district would have been considered negligent for inadequate supervision.

Bob's first reaction was to report the problem to the superintendent. Undoubtedly, Ron would have called his board committee members and the result would have been a strong memo sent to the union. Such a step might well be necessary, but he knew that it would not help the overall situation. He had to think about possible alternatives for dealing with the problem.

This was only one of the dilemmas he faced. The union had decided to wear black buttons inscribed with the word "Why?" The "Why?" button represented the question, "why was there no teachers' contract?" Most teachers had been wearing these buttons during class for several weeks without causing any problem. Now there was a taxpayer group who had made their own buttons which said "Because!" and it was rumored that a group of students were going to wear these new buttons to school. Bob knew some of the more militant teachers might become upset with these button-sporting students and that some kind of confrontation was possible. Someone else had told him that one of the custodians was also planning to wear a "Because!" button to school.

Not only were there differences between students, staff, and faculty, but the teachers themselves were not all of a like mind. One teacher, who was not supporting the union tactics, had come into the building before the parking lot meeting and procession and found a little sign taped on her mailbox which read "Scab." The teacher was furious and confronted one of the leaders of the union in the high school office. This led to an angry shouting match which was witnessed by the secretaries and several students. Bob's secretary had reported the incident to him, but he had yet to act.

That was still not the worst of it. Bob had also heard a rumor that in ten days the union was planning to picket the high school's fall concert. It was to be a peaceful demonstration during which union members would distribute a pamphlet explaining their position in the negotiations. He knew that many parents would not appreciate the picketing. Until this crisis, teachers had generally been respected by members of the community, but now there were indications that many citizens had little sympathy for them. Even though faculty salaries in the district were below the median level in the county, many residents were taking home considerably less pay than the experienced teachers. As in every district, there were also a few teachers who were thought to be incompetent and many residents felt they should be fired and should certainly not receive a raise. While the Board of Education had cleverly used the school newsletter to argue its position, the union had no comparable communication method and had decided on the informational picket.

Bob knew that the superintendent had not yet heard about the plans to picket. As soon as he did, there was little question that some sort of confrontation was likely. Although the district could attempt to stop the picketing with a court order, a more emotional confrontation in front of his school was the likely possibility. As he pulled into his driveway, Bob knew that he had to put these problems aside, at least until after dinner and his household quieted down. At about 10:00, he left his wife watching television and went to his den to think about his problems.

## POSSIBLE DISCUSSION QUESTIONS

1. As a respected principal and member of the community, should Bob attempt to intervene in any way in the negotiations? If so, what should he do?

2. What should he do about the faculty coming in late after their meetings in the parking lot?

3. What should he do about the buttons?

4. What should be his reaction to the confrontation which took place in his outer office?

5. What, if anything, should he do about the rumored picketing at the fall concert?

# Case Study 2

# A Moral and Legal Dilemma

What is morally and legally acceptable in our society is constantly changing. An appropriate response to a moral or ethical problem can also depend on community standards. In addition, when faced with an issue that could have legal implications, a school administrator must become familiar with the status of the law related to the problem. Administrators must also be sensitive to the impact their words and actions have upon individual employees, parents, and students.

Sally Lyons had been assistant superintendent of schools for personnel for eleven years and had worked with three different superintendents. Earlier in her career, she had the opportunity to be appointed the superintendent, but had preferred to remain in her present position. For Sally, nothing was more important in the school district than hiring the best possible personnel and maintaining programs that ensure all employees find their work rewarding and challenging. At this point, the district seemed to be functioning effectively with a new superintendent. Sally looked at Bill Kison almost as a son, and she knew that since arriving in the district he had relied on her heavily for difficult decisions. She did not doubt her ability to help lead the school system through any crisis, but a call that she had just received that morning had somewhat shaken her.

Betty Crossetti, an elementary principal in the district, had presented her with a dilemma. One of her middle school teachers, Karen Glass, an English teacher in her second year, had informed Betty that she was two months pregnant, which is not a particularly surprising announcement in a profession where close to seventy percent of the practitioners are women. What was upsetting about Karen's situation was that the young teacher was not married and had no plans for a wedding in the near future. She told her principal that although she and her boyfriend, both under twenty-five and from broken homes, were living together, they were not yet ready to commit to a lifelong relationship. Although the fact that Karen and her boyfriend were living together in the district had been brought to the attention of the administration by several concerned parents, this new development would undoubtedly upset many more residents.

The school district of 3,000 students was primarily rural and conservative. Many of the community leaders were evangelical Christians and members of local Baptist and Free Methodist churches. Three church leaders were also members of the Board of Education. These board members frequently expressed concern about moral and ethical questions faced by the school district. Sally still remembered the emotional discussions about adding sex education to the health curriculum. After the course syllabus had finally been agreed upon and approved by the board, the health teacher had invited a representative of Planned Parenthood to speak to the classes. Because the Board of Education's position stressed abstinence, Planned Parenthood's class presentation had reignited the conflict and was a major factor leading to the denial of tenure to the health teacher.

Sally remembered that Karen, the teacher in question, was doing a good job in the classroom. The reviews of the principal had all been positive and suggested that Karen was an energetic, creative, if somewhat emotional young lady whose only defect seemed to be an oversensitivity to constructive criticism. Also, she was one of the most popular teachers in the middle school. Even with this positive beginning as a probationary teacher, Karen was still one year away from being eligible for tenure.

Upon hearing of Karen's pregnancy, her principal had immediately called Sally to ask her to speak with the young teacher. Within minutes, Karen would be sitting in Sally's office telling her story. How should Sally react? What were the options? Sally began to make some notes:

1. She could be neutral in her response and merely say that she would discuss the issue with the superintendent. Sally knew that the district would have to obtain a legal opinion on the issue before taking any action.
2. She could be sympathetic and offer the young teacher at least some advice and encouragement.

Thinking about what she might say, Betty knew she would have to share the problem with the superintendent. As a newcomer to the district, he might be unaware of some of the historic problems and would have some difficulty gauging the possible community reaction. In any case, he would seek Betty's counsel and advice. As she pondered, her secretary rang to announce that Miss Glass was here to see her. Betty reached into her drawer and took out the box of tissues, as she expected this to be a difficult interview.

## POSSIBLE DISCUSSION QUESTIONS

1. How should Betty deal with the conference she is about to begin?
2. What line of action should she recommend to the superintendent?

*Case Study 3*

# The Decision

Of all the decisions that must be made by a superintendent of schools, perhaps the most difficult is deciding when to close school because of weather conditions. This problem often plagues administrators in colder climates, but weather can create a crisis anywhere. A wrong decision can create serious consequences for an administrator and because accidents can occur during bad weather, parents are particularly sensitive about a superintendent's decisions regarding school closings. On the other hand, the superintendent can also be criticized if school is closed too often for no apparent reason. How does an administrator make such a decision? What happens when he or she is wrong?

James Wilson was in his fourteenth year as superintendent of the Hillsdale School District. For the most part, they had been good years for him and his growing family. At age 37, he didn't expect to spend his entire career in this small, rural district, but he was gaining valuable experience and would soon be ready to consider a larger school district. At 5:10 A.M. on this particular morning, James wasn't thinking about the distant future, he was looking out his office window thinking about the weather. He couldn't see much, but he knew that the ground was bare and there wasn't a snowflake in sight. He had come in early because the weather report on the late news had predicted a snowstorm during the next twenty-four hours. The forecaster had said that snow would "most likely" arrive in the Hillsdale area sometime in the afternoon. James thought back to the previous year when there had been a similar prediction. With great fanfare, the weathermen had predicted a large storm and schools and even some businesses closed in anticipation of its arrival. But except for a few scattered flurries, it missed the city and the superintendents in the area often joked about the storm that never came. Still, James and the others were well aware that on most days, the weather forecasters were quite accurate.

James had set his alarm for 4:45 A.M. this morning and after plugging in the coffeepot, he turned on the kitchen radio and looked out the window. It was calm,

6

but the first forecast of the day was still predicting a storm from the west that would reach the local area sometime in the afternoon. James noted that while the announcer talked about a "storm warning" for the entire area, the word "blizzard" was never used. He wondered what the difference was between a storm and a blizzard, but expected that a storm could be bad enough. Normally on a stormy morning, James would get in his car and inspect the district conditions. He would also call the local highway department for a report and check with the sheriff's office. After that, he would meet with the school's director of transportation and make a decision. If possible, this was done no later than 5:30 A.M., so that the bus drivers were not forced to drive in the storm.

Today, there was no reason to drive through the district or call anyone. James thought about phoning another local superintendent who might have gone through days like this before, but decided not to bother his colleague. Instead, he had driven directly to his office to meet with Pete Woodlane, the director of transportation. Pete was not particularly helpful in making these decisions, and James knew that in the end, it would be his call. It was obvious that the weather was fine now, but if the forecast was correct, the area was likely to have a real storm. Again, he listened to several local radio stations to get an updated forecast. Everyone was still talking about "the storm" that was likely to come this afternoon. People driving to work were told to expect a tough ride home.

It certainly didn't sound good, but as the sun approached the horizon, James could not remember a clearer or more beautiful morning. After a brief conversation with the director of transportation, James went to his own office with the promise that they would talk again in ten minutes. Sitting there looking out the window, James knew he had a difficult decision to make and that he would have to make it soon. Since whatever he did could turn out to be wrong, he decided to keep some notes on "the decision."

**5:20 A.M.** The radio station continued to talk about a "storm warning" for the afternoon. To the west, "there was much snowing and blowing," but snowing and blowing had been part of the weather pattern in this area at least fifty days a year. Still, when the local station announced the first school closing, I began to worry. My friend Larry Delsing, in a neighboring district, had closed his district for the day. Of course, we always kidded Larry for being a "nervous Nelly," who closed at the first sign of snow. The second decision to close was Charlotte Nellest, a bright, young, new superintendent in Linhurst, a district to the south. Even with this closing, it was still only two of the ten districts in the county. I knew that the other superintendents were also struggling with their decision.

**5:25 A.M.** After a brief conversation with Pete Woodlane, I decided not to cancel school, at least not at this point. This meant that the drivers would be on their way to school.

**6:00 A.M.** Almost all the drivers were here and there was still no sign of snow or wind. As the sun came up, the calm was almost eerie. People going to work were moving along at a normal speed. This time, when the radio station announced the school closings, five of the ten county schools had closed. The weather report had not changed. I then took a walk to the bus drivers' lounge. (Lounge might be too glamorous a characterization, for it was merely a partitioned section of the boiler room.) The drivers were in a good mood, but all of them were talking about the weather report. When I asked one of the drivers whether we should go out, he replied that days like this were the reason superintendents got paid the "big bucks." John Smith, a veteran driver, suggested that I call it off and said, "You will take more grief for having the kids out in a storm than you would get for keeping them home." On the other hand, I knew that "snow days" caused a crisis for many working parents as they would have to quickly seek baby-sitting for their young children. It was clear that there was no way I was going to win on this decision.

**6:10 A.M.** As I returned to my office, all of the phones were ringing. Even though they had been told to listen to the radio, parents and students were calling to find out if school was canceled. I answered a few of the calls and then decided to let the phones ring. The number of county school closes was still only five out of the ten. At that point, I really wanted to talk to someone, so I tried to get through to another county superintendent whom I liked and respected. Although Bob Smith liked to give the impression that he was a "tough guy," he was sensitive and competent. He told me that he was going to send out the buses, as he had been panicked by the weathermen last year and was not going to fall into the same trap again. I had been leaning towards canceling school, but as Bob pointed out, we could still dismiss school early, before the storm reached our area.

**6:25 A.M.** The sun was up and it was a beautiful winter day. Pete Woodlane, the director of transportation, called to remind me that the first buses needed to leave by 6:30 A.M. I knew that once the buses were out on the road, I would be committed to the decision. I thought it would be helpful to have more time, but I knew the weather would not change in the next hour. Finally, I looked out the window at the sunshine and called Pete and told him to "send them out."

**6:45 A.M.** After the buses were all out on the road, three more of the city districts had called in their closings to the radio stations. That meant that Bob and I were the only superintendents to send out our buses. If we were wrong, we could be in big trouble.

**7:45 A.M.** The middle school and high school students were now all in their buildings and Pete called to make sure I wanted to send out the buses on the second run to pick up the elementary students. It would look very strange if I now decided to cancel school for the elementary students, so I told him to "bring them in." Once more, I turned on the radio and although the weather report had not changed, the forecast was now suggesting that the storm might reach our area "in the middle of the afternoon." It occurred to me that I could relieve my morning-long tension headache by sending all the students home at 10:00 A.M.

**9:15 A.M.** On my way to the high school office, it seemed the noise level in the halls was higher than usual. Students were talking about the weather and several students asked me good-naturedly, "When are we going home?" I joked that I didn't want to send them home with the possibility of a storm, and suggested that we might all stay the night. One disgruntled faculty member was not nearly so amiable when he remarked "everybody else is closed, what are we still doing here?" I felt a tinge of anger, but decided to leave the question unanswered.

**10:30 A.M.** After a productive meeting on an upcoming staff development day, I headed back to my office. I must admit that during the meeting, I forgot all about the weather. When I arrived in my office, I could see that the sun had disappeared and the wind had picked up. The forecast on the radio had changed and the announcer was using the dreaded words "blizzard conditions for this afternoon." I quickly phoned the director of transportation and told him to call the drivers in as soon as possible. They had been told to remain close to the phone and to be ready for early dismissal. The high school principal was notified that the buses would be ready in about forty-five minutes. Mrs. Jones, my secretary, notified me that we were getting dozens of calls from parents asking when we were going to dismiss the students. She mentioned that some of the comments were quite "uncomplimentary" to the superintendent. Mrs. Jones was asked to inform the radio station, and any parents who called, that we would be dismissing at 11:00 A.M. Three of the drivers were still not in. I told the director of transportation to have the buses brought to the loading area and to call in substitute drivers if necessary. When the announcement of the early dismissal was made on the public address system, a large cheer could be heard throughout the school.

**11:10 A.M.** We were finally ready for dismissal. It was dark and the winds had become very strong. I decided it was time for a couple of aspirins.

**11:25 A.M.** What was to be known as the "Blizzard of 1977" had arrived. All of a sudden, as I looked out the window, all I could see was blinding snow. Visibility was close to zero and most of the buses still had not delivered all of their children home. Using the radio, we instructed the drivers to find a safe place and get off of the road.

**12:15 P.M.** Two buses reported that they were indeed off the road, but stuck in snow. The weather had not yet let up. Jane Leash, the elementary principal, called and I advised her to prepare to stay as long as necessary. We would not dismiss the elementary children during this storm.

**1:00 P.M.** If anything, the weather was worse. The sheriff announced on the radio that there should be no "unnecessary travel." Our school district had seventeen buses stranded in the middle of this blizzard, and there was no question that I was responsible.

**1:30 P.M.** We instructed the drivers that, if possible, they and their students should try to make it to a nearby home or building, but not to attempt this if it would endanger anyone. We now had at least six inches of snow, although with the high winds it was difficult to tell.

**2:30 P.M.** The elementary principal was asked to begin to formulate a plan for spending the night. The cafeteria staff had to be asked to use whatever food was available to feed the students supper, as well as breakfast.

**4:30 P.M.** Reports had been coming in from the bus drivers. It appeared that the drivers and children had all found shelter. Some were in churches, others in the town hall, and a number were in private homes. One family had seventeen extra guests for supper that night, but at least everyone was safe. I was not sure about some of the high school faculty who had left immediately after the buses, but there were at least a dozen teachers left in the building who were prepared to spend the night with several stranded students. Everyone seemed to be having a good time. I decided that it was my place to join the 775 elementary students and their faculty who were having a "sleepover." Before I left, I phoned the radio stations to announce that the students were all accounted for and safe. (I also received a call from my wife that the water pipes above the bathroom had frozen and she was without water.)

**7:00 A.M. (next day)** I finally got to sleep at 4:30 A.M. With the exception of a couple of children who cried because they wanted to go home, the evening went quite well. The cafeteria staff made peanut butter and jelly sandwiches and we had carrot sticks, milk, and ice cream. After several hours of movies in the auditorium, the teachers and students settled on the floors of their classrooms for a night they would all remember. By 12:30 A.M., the school seemed quiet and I sat down with the elementary principal to talk about the next day. We decided that we would ask the town and village to help us get our buses to the school by sending the plows out in front of them. After loading the children and with a plow leading the way, we would get the children home if and when the weather cleared. Elementary teachers would be asked to supervise the bus trip home. The phones continued to ring most of the night and a number of parents used their snowmobiles to pick up their children. We instituted a sign-out process to help us keep track of who had left. During the early morning hours, more parents showed up in the office. Although it was still snowing and we now had close to twenty inches, most parents were in a decent frame of mind and there was an air of excitement about the whole adventure. A breakfast of peanut butter and jelly sandwiches and juice was served, and then the buses were loaded and began their slow, torturous journey to take the children home to their anxious parents.

**5:30 A.M.** The report just came in that the last bus was back to school safely. I personally thanked all of the faculty and staff members who had helped us through the ordeal.

**6:15 A.M.** I shook hands with the elementary principal and set out for my own home, where my family was bearing up well without either water or electrical power.

## THE AFTERMATH

Four days have passed and school is still not in session. James has remained home with his family to wait for the roads to be cleared so he can return to school. He is aware that at the next Board of Education meeting he will have to talk about his decision to have school on the day of the storm. Even though there were no injuries and everyone is now safely at home, he is certain that many will criticize his decision. James is not sure what he should say to the board and feels fortunate that he has some time to think about how he should deal with the issue. Unfortunately, he won't have the luxury of deciding how to react to the criticism: As he was making lunch for his family, he received a phone call from a reporter at the local newspaper. The reporter informed James that a group of citizens were circulating a petition to be presented at next week's Board of Education meeting. The petition calls for the board to dismiss the superintendent for his "reckless and indefensible" decision to hold school on the day of a predicted blizzard. The reporter wanted to get James's comment on the petition.

## POSSIBLE DISCUSSION QUESTIONS

1. Looking back on "the decision," was the superintendent justified in making the decision that he did?

2. Is there anything he can do to improve his decision making process on potential snowdays in the future?

3. What should James say to the reporter?

4. How should he deal with the issue at the upcoming Board of Education meeting?

# Case Study 4

# Appointing a Chairperson

Selecting the right person to carry out leadership and management functions is a major responsibility of superintendents and principals. It is an especially sensitive task when the primary candidates are from within the system. In any hiring decision, candidates have varied strengths and weaknesses and administrators must determine what characteristics are most essential for the position in question.

Everyone was expecting that John Pearlman would retire this year, so the official announcement came as no surprise. John had been social studies coordinator for the Bridgeport District for twenty-three years. In addition to his administrative responsibilities, he had also taught two sections of advanced placement American history. As both a teacher and an administrator, he had been outstanding. During his career, he had helped to select all eleven of the district's social studies teachers. The coordinator was also responsible for social studies curriculums in grades K through 12, so John also had many friends in the district's two elementary schools as well.

As soon as his retirement became public, faculty members throughout the district began to talk about a possible successor. Speculation was centered on two members of the department who were known to be very interested in the position.

Superintendent Lou Banks knew both of these two individuals quite well. He and the four building principals who would be involved in the decision were well aware of the strengths and weaknesses of each potential candidate. A second member of the department was retiring as well, so they could also seek an outside candidate to assume the leadership of the department.

Within a week after the retirement announcement, both Vincent Kennely and Sally Williams wrote the superintendent letters expressing their interest in the position. Superintendent Banks was quite certain that if the students were consulted, Mr. Kennely would undoubtedly be their choice. A charismatic actor in the classroom, his European history classes were famous throughout the district and brought history to life. His teaching featured many creative projects that always maintained a high level of student interest. Mr. Kennely could also motivate students to participate in his Model United Nations Club, one of the strongest and most active in the state. He was the kind of teacher who inspired students to attend college to become social studies teachers. His excellent sense of humor and concern for young people made him an extremely popular teacher and students would come to his room during free periods or after school just to talk. As a chairperson, Mr. Kennely would undoubtedly take a sincere interest in young teachers and help them succeed. There was no question that during his eleven years in the district, he had earned the respect of his fellow faculty members and the community for his innovative teaching. Mr. Banks also expected Mr. Kennely could help his colleagues at the elementary school develop creative ways to teach social studies in their classrooms.

On the other hand, the superintendent had talked enough with Mr. Kennely's principal to know that this excellent teacher had some weaknesses. He was often late in completing necessary paperwork and had shown little interest in either the scheduling or the budget process. His classroom, although very colorful and filled with historic displays, appeared disorganized, and his filing system was, to say the least, unique. When asked about these potential weaknesses, Mr. Kennely said that he was sure he could learn the mechanical aspects of the chairperson's job. Given the opportunity to vote, at least five members of the department would probably support Mr. Kennely. In his letter to the superintendent, he had made clear that he was committed to working with his colleagues at all levels to improve the social studies program in the Bridgeport District.

Sally Williams was equally confident that she could be an effective leader of the department. An active faculty member, she had successfully chaired many school-wide committees. In addition, she had risen to a leadership position in the state social studies organization, and as its current secretary, she would automatically become the president in two years. Active in state level curriculum work, Mrs. Williams had spent several summers developing a new social studies program for middle schools throughout the state.

Unlike Mr. Kennely, Mrs. Williams always completed reports on time and had been active on scheduling and budget committees. Her classroom and files were in excellent order and no one doubted her skills both as a manager and facilitator. On the other hand, unlike Mr. Kennely, who always appeared relaxed, Mrs. Williams sometimes seemed very intense and although her colleagues respected her, they were not always comfortable with her. She was extremely well organized in the classroom, but quite traditional in her teaching methods and more concerned than Mr. Kennely about the standardized testing results of her students. At the same time, Mrs. Williams regularly read professional journals and would occasionally try new methods suggested in the articles. She was not unpopular with students or other faculty, but she certainly did not have the kind of following which supported Mr. Kennely.

Considering his options, the superintendent thought about the possibility of hiring an outsider to fill the position. If he advertised for a department social studies coordinator, he was certain there would be a large number of applicants. At the same time, he strongly suspected that both the teachers in the department and the faculty as a whole would prefer that someone be appointed from within the district. Although the social studies teachers might be divided on their first choice, he expected they all would accept either Mr. Kennely or Mrs. Williams. A decision to seek an outside candidate would demonstrate to some teachers a lack of confidence in the current faculty. Superintendent Banks could just hear the union president asking him, "Don't you believe in promoting from within?" An outsider might have all of the strengths of both candidates, but that was far from certain.

There was another concern that he perhaps should consider. Of the seven subject area coordinators, only one was a woman, and three of the four principals were male. With a district faculty that was seventy-five percent women, he knew the Board of Education had been criticized for repeatedly choosing males for leadership roles.

What did the school district need? A solid and effective manager who would keep the department on a steady course, or a charismatic leader who might inspire his fellow teachers to new heights? Or should the alternative of recruiting a person who fills both roles be pursued?

## POSSIBLE DISCUSSION QUESTIONS

1. If you were the superintendent of the district, what process would you follow in selecting the new social studies coordinator?

2. What traits do you feel are most important for a position such as the one described in this case study?

3. Should the gender of the candidate be considered in making the decision?

4. How important should the opinions of the four principals be in helping the superintendent make a decision?

5. Should the superintendent personally consult with the other members of the department?

*Case Study 5*

# The Residence Requirement

Should a school administrator be required to live in the district in which he or she works? Board members and parents often support the idea that their principals and superintendents should live and participate in the community and that they should send their children to district schools. On the other hand, many administrators worry about the effects such residency requirements can have on their personal lives and on their families. It can be extremely inconvenient for a family to move to a new community, especially if a spouse has a job in their current one. Sometimes an administrator's children can resist any move that interrupts their education and established friendships, and parents also worry about the pressure that results from being the child of an administrator. In this case study, the superintendent and the Board of Education are struggling with the residence requirement issue for the new middle school principal they are hiring.

Ben Westgate had lived and worked in Lansingville for thirty-five years. Following graduation from the local teachers' college, he married and a month later accepted an English teacher position in the high school. His three children had graduated from the high school and both he and his wife were active in numerous community organizations, as well as the local Presbyterian church. After he was promoted to high school principal and then named superintendent of schools, he and his family had never even considered leaving the community. It was a good life and his entire family had prospered in the school district. As superintendent, he was expected to be active in the community, and his annual evaluation by the Board of Education included a section on community involvement. Now, with the middle school principal position vacant, he and the board members were grappling with whether or not this position description would include a residence requirement.

Ben knew that a majority of the Board of Education wanted to include such a requirement. Lansingville was a relatively poor rural district and the middle

15

school principal would be one of the highest paid people in the community. Cindy Tripp, a veteran member of the board, had said to him that for $65,000 a year, it was not too much to ask that a principal live and participate in the community. The superintendent was well aware that one of the reasons for the current dilemma was Bruce Kinder, the outgoing principal. Bruce had been a competent and effective leader. He had attended board meetings when invited and had occasionally been seen at school events. There was little question, however, that his personal life was lived thirty miles away in a suburban community. His wife, Helen, worked in a law firm in the city and was almost never seen in Lansingville. Their children attended a parochial school and had seldom visited Lansingville Middle School. Bruce came to school and did his job and went back to the suburbs to live his life.

A young man on his way up, Bruce saw Lansingville as just a stop along the way and he had accepted a position as assistant superintendent in a nearby suburban district. Some board members and parents felt that he had been a "carpetbagger" who had never really belonged to the community, and that for him, the principalship of Lansingville Middle School was "just a job." A number of people in the community wanted someone who would be at church suppers, parades in the village, and take their turn being president of the local Kiwanis Club. For board member John Schultz, "a school principal should be someone you could call at home in the evening if you had an urgent problem." Bruce Kinder even had an unlisted telephone number. With the exception of the professional staff at school, the district had very few people with college educations and there was an underlying feeling in the village that these highly paid professionals should be paying school taxes to the district. The conventional wisdom was that if school administrators were paying property taxes, they might spend district money more carefully. Several board members were also critical of the former principal for attending conferences and meetings. In their view, there were plenty of meetings he could have attended to help out within the community.

Ben Westgate did not disagree with most of these sentiments and believed he was a more effective superintendent because he lived in the community. On the other hand, he knew that many other administrators disagreed with him. Approximately thirty-three percent of the superintendents in the county did not live in the school district in which they worked. The percentage of principals living outside their district was probably even larger. Increasingly, new administrators were hesitant to accept contracts that contained a residence requirement. There was no question in Ben's mind that requiring the new principal to reside in the district would reduce the pool of applicants for the job. He also expected that two current faculty members who lived outside the district would not apply for the position if they were forced to move. One of these individuals could be a finalist for the job.

Ben wondered whether it was better to take a slightly less qualified candidate if that person was willing to move into the district and become an active participant in school and community affairs. Neither of the other two building principals lived in the community, but both did a better job than Bruce had done in coming back to the school district in the evenings and on weekends. He could not help but wonder how these two principals would react to a residence requirement in the middle school principal job description.

It was clear to Ben that unless he took a strong position against it, the Board of Education would insist on the requirement. The agenda for the next meeting, along with supporting materials that included the proposed job description, had to be sent out this afternoon. He could procrastinate no longer.

## POSSIBLE DISCUSSION QUESTIONS

1. Should the superintendent include the residence requirement on the job description he is preparing for the Board?

2. If he decides not to include it, how will he defend his position at the upcoming meeting?

3. If he does include it, how should he handle the situation with the two remaining principals?

4. Do you think that it is wise for an administrator to live in the district in which he or she works?

## Case Study 6

# Request for a Leave of Absence

Sometimes what is best for a faculty or staff member is not necessarily best for the school district. In this case, the faculty member is requesting a leave of absence for personal reasons. Leave requests are not uncommon in school districts and the conditions for such leaves are often enumerated in a union contract or Board of Education policy. Occasionally, requests will occur which are not covered, and the administration must make a recommendation to the Board of Education as to whether such a request should be granted.

For six years, Linda Woods had been an effective high school physics and chemistry teacher, but this past year had been difficult for her. Not only had she been out of school twenty-three days for illness, but her personal life seemed to be in shambles. She had recently been through an emotional divorce and had been depressed for most of the year. Though there had been no children involved, the ending of her marriage continued to plague her throughout the school year. Linda's friends on the faculty were able to convince her to seek out professional counseling. Her counselor, along with a close friend, had helped her prepare a letter to the Board of Education.

That letter now sat on the desk of the high school principal, Sandra Denson. What the letter requested was unique in Sandra's experience as an administrator. The teacher was asking for a one-year leave of absence for "personal reasons." During the discussion with Sandra, Linda had said she wanted to go home for a year to live with her parents. She believed she needed to get away completely from both the community and her former husband. Linda also admitted to Sandra that she had developed a drinking problem during the last year and she thought that living at home would help her deal with this difficulty more effectively. Her principal was very sure after the interview that Linda needed to do something to get her life together.

During her first five years on the faculty, Linda had been one of the two or three best teachers at the high school; both students and colleagues had respected her as a teacher and as a human being. On the other hand, the preponderance of tears during their talk indicated Linda was in no condition to be in the classroom. As her immediate supervisor, Sandra felt compelled to ask whether Linda thought she would ever want to come back and teach in the district. The young teacher had been unable to answer the question and it seemed to only upset her further. After this meeting with Linda, Sandra knew if the leave request was denied, Linda would feel even more alone and abandoned.

The chemistry-physics position in the school had always been very difficult to fill. The job required dual certification in both subjects and even though the vacancy had been advertised throughout the state, there had only been two certified candidates at the time Linda was hired. There was little question that the market for dually certified science teachers had not improved during the past six years. It occurred to Sandra that if the leave were granted, the district could only offer a one-year contract to the new teacher, which would make recruitment even more difficult. Even if her job were saved for her, it certainly seemed possible that Linda would still be in a depressed state a year from now. If the leave were denied, it would allow the school to start fresh with a teacher unencumbered by the emotional problems that plagued Linda. In any case, it would be much easier to find a qualified person for a permanent position than to find someone to accept a job which might only last for a year.

Feeling great empathy for Linda, Sandra was torn. If Linda could solve her personal problems, her professional abilities could lead to a distinguished career as a science teacher. It was conceivable that she could someday be a principal or a superintendent. Sandra knew she wanted to support the request for the leave, but was that really what was right for the school?

As the principal considered the problem, she knew that the superintendent and possibly the Board of Education would have a number of questions concerning the leave request. Her answers to these inquiries would affect their final decision. They would probably ask her if she thought Linda would really return after a year and whether going home to her parents would solve her problems. Another concern was likely to be whether the district was creating a new precedent in granting such a leave, and they would certainly want to know how likely it was that a qualified substitute could be found for the coming year.

Sandra did not have any definite answers for any of these questions, but she knew Linda's letter must be shared with the superintendent, who would then want to know her opinion on the matter.

## POSSIBLE DISCUSSION QUESTIONS

1. What should be the primary factors considered in making a decision on this request?

2. Is there any alternative to saying either "yes" or "no" to the request?

3. What position would you take as an administrator, given what you know about this case?

# What to Do about the Basketball Coach

Millions of people watch high school basketball each year and in most communities the basketball coach is a well-known public figure. Sports booster clubs, alumni, and parents of team members carefully monitor a coach's behavior and decisions. If the team wins, people are usually supportive, but even victory does not save a coach from his or her critics. Decisions on who should play, as well as game strategy, can be a source of widespread discussion. Unrest among team members can be a major issue, and school administrators frequently receive complaints by community members and parents. In this case study, the superintendent's key advisors disagree on the coach's merits. In the end, the superintendent will have to make a decision.

Bob Benson had been through this before. Five years ago, during the first year of his tenure as superintendent, a large number of community members had been upset with the varsity basketball coach, Bill Turner. Even though there were no serious charges against the coach at the time, the team had had three consecutive losing seasons. Over thirty members of the sports booster club had attended a Board of Education meeting and the group had been granted an executive session with the board to discuss the coach. Although they had described him as a "nice guy," he had limited knowledge of the game, had not played college basketball, and had only mediocre basketball skills himself. They cited such incidents as failing to call a critical time-out during the final minutes of a game, and allowing a star player with four fouls to continue playing in the game. When the boy fouled out, critics said Coach Turner should have saved him for the second half. Some complained that he failed to properly teach and develop a 6'8" center who could have made a real contribution to the team, while others charged that the coach was "too easy" on the boys. Practices were too relaxed, and according to some, the team lacked intensity when playing the game.

Bob, the other administrators, and the faculty were supportive of the coach, but when it became clear that a majority of the Board of Education felt that a change in coaches was advisable, Bob had encouraged Coach Turner to look elsewhere. When an assistant coaching position suddenly opened at the local community college, he had strongly suggested that the coach seek the job. Partially because of his guilt in the matter, Bob had worked hard to influence some friends at the college to select Coach Turner for the position. Although it was less money, the new job had resolved what could have been a major conflict in the school district.

Bob remembered that in selecting a replacement coach, the administration had gone out of its way to find someone who would be acceptable to the critics. Jim O'Connor was a 6'4" ex-Marine who had had a successful college basketball career. His physical education classes were known for their strict discipline, and while he had never resorted to physical force, there was little question that some students were intimidated by him.

As the new basketball coach, it was soon evident that Coach O'Connor would be demanding and strict with his players. Any member of the team who was late or missed practice was severely disciplined. Unlike the previous coach, he sought respect, not friendship, from the students. During his first year, the team had a winning season and most of the people in the community were supportive of his efforts. This year, due in part to some early season injuries, the team had lost its first four games. Coach O'Connor began calling Saturday practices and working the players harder than ever. As the season continued, he made fewer substitutions and in some games only seven boys played. Community members began to hear stories of how the coach was always yelling at the team, and several players commented publicly that being on the team was no longer fun.

With the season almost over, the team's record was four and eleven, and the spirit and size of crowds at the games seemed to be dwindling. While all of the administration members were aware of the dissatisfaction among players, parents, and members of the booster club, none of them were ready for the letter containing over fifty signatures that had arrived yesterday, addressed to the superintendent. Copies had also been sent to the high school principal, Pam Schultz, and the athletic director, Art Conlin. Bob pulled the letter out of his top drawer and read it for the third time.

Dear Mr. Benson,

The undersigned parents, students, and community members have grave concerns about our varsity basketball coach Mr. O'Connor. We would cite the following problems which are plaguing our team.

1. *Poor morale*—of the thirteen members of the team, only seven have played during four out of the last five games. Coach O'Connor expects everyone to work hard at practice, but does not reward the hard work by giving team members playing time. No one feels that they can talk to the coach about this or any other issue because he seems to be unapproachable. Even those team members who are playing say that they are not enjoying being on the team this year. Many of the players feel that it is like being in military basic training.

2. *Fear of making a mistake*—both at practice and during games, players are afraid of being yelled at. This causes them to be tentative in the way they play.

3. *The conservative nature of the type of basketball being taught*—with the coach's emphasis on defense and working only for a "good shot," much of the fun of the game has been taken away for the players and spectators. The boys want to "run the floor" and use the fast break whenever possible. Coach O'Connor's deliberate style of play is not nearly as enjoyable to play or to watch as was the "wide open style" used in the past.

4. *The coach is unbending and has unnecessarily harsh rules*—for example, the other day a student was three minutes late for practice because he was talking with a teacher. The player was made to run fifty laps around the gym. Another illustration was when a substitute player forgot to bring his warm-up pants for a game. He was not allowed to participate or even dress for the game.

These are just a few of the concerns we have about Mr. O'Connor. For this reason, we would like to invite you to a private meeting to be held at the American Legion Hall, February 21st, at 7:30. This meeting will give concerned students, parents, and interested community members the opportunity to share with you first hand other examples of the problems with our varsity basketball program. Rather than take this issue directly to the Board of Education, we thought such a meeting would be helpful. As the situation now stands, we feel that it would be unacceptable if Mr. O'Connor were to be recommended for another year as our varsity basketball coach.

P.S. We would ask that you not share the names of those who signed this letter with Mr. O'Connor.

There were fifty-three signatures, including those of nine varsity basketball players. Most of their parents had also signed, along with the president of the sports booster club and two of the other five officers of the organization.

Bob was waiting for the athletic director and the principal to join him to discuss an appropriate reaction to this letter. Bob knew the coach was a pleasant man in social situations, and well liked by faculty. This popularity would ensure that the faculty union would actively oppose any attempt to terminate him as the coach. As for his advisors, he already knew what they were going to say. Principal Pam Schultz would be sympathetic with the critics, as she had always found Mr. O'Connor to be a difficult staff member. She knew that Mr. O'Connor felt the basketball team was more important than any other school program. When one of his substitute players, a fine trumpet player, asked to be excused from a game to play in an all-county music concert, the coach had told him to make a choice. If music was his priority, then he would have to give up basketball. Such a rigid position had brought the coach into conflict with his principal, and when she tried to reason with him, he had threatened to resign.

On the other hand, Art Conlin, the athletic director, was extremely supportive of Coach O'Connor. A veteran member of the faculty, he had heard complaints about coaches for fifteen years. Art was afraid that if the school fired every coach that was criticized by the public, it would be impossible to fill the coaching vacancies in the district. On first hearing the letter, he had said to the superintendent:

> Some of these guys who think they know so much about basketball wouldn't last two weeks as a coach with today's kids. The kids on our basketball team this year need to be taught discipline. They are a group of complainers who don't even seem to like each other. Last year, when we had a winning season and a couple of seniors were leaders on the team, no one talked about morale problems. Now is the time we must support the coach. We should tell these people what they can do with their letter.

Bob knew all of this would come out again in his meeting with the principal and the athletic director. He also knew it would be his decision as to how to react to the letter.

## POSSIBLE DISCUSSION QUESTIONS

1. How should the superintendent structure his meeting with the principal and the athletic director?

2. What, if anything, should the coach be told about the letter?

3. Should the Board of Education be informed?

4. Should the union leadership be told about the letter?

5. What should the superintendent do about the invitation to attend the meeting at the American Legion? If the invitation is not accepted, what reason should be given? If the superintendent accepts the invitation, should he invite the principal and athletic director to attend?

6. If he does accept the invitation, what should be the strategy of the superintendent at the meeting?

# The Athletic Director's Dilemma

Schools tend to have many policies and rules, and the enforcement of these regulations can create ethical dilemmas for school administrators. While flexibility is sometimes required, an administrator must guard against arbitrary and inequitable decisions. There are also times when leaders are faced with decisions they might choose to avoid. In the following situation, the school athletic director must either help to enforce a rule that he disagrees with, or make a decision that he might someday regret.

Bob Lewis was sitting in his office on the morning of one of the most important basketball games in the history of Greeley Central School. Greeley was the smallest school in its division, and in the twenty-seven years since the division's formation, a boys' basketball team from Greeley had never made it to the regional state basketball finals. They would be playing a crucial game tonight and victory would place them in the state championship tournament. The entire community was excited about the team that had a nineteen and one record thus far this year. Fans were turned away from recent home games, and although it was being played in a nearby city high school, tonight's game was also expected to be a sellout.

Students and faculty would converge on the gym for a pep rally this afternoon, where Bob would be speaking, along with the varsity coach, Sid Lindsay. He had been preparing his remarks for the rally when he received a call from Janet Smith, the secretary in the high school office. Bob now wished that he had been anyplace but his office when the call came through, because the news was the last thing he wanted to hear. Janet told him that at 10:08 A.M. Billy Lyons, the 6'7" center on the basketball team, had only just arrived at school. Friends since high school, Janet had decided to call Bob before sharing the news with her immediate supervisor, the high school principal, Jim Hensel. If Billy Lyons' tardiness was reported to the principal, it would undoubtedly make Billy ineligible to play in tonight's game. As an all-conference all star this year, Billy had averaged twenty-four points and eleven rebounds a game. Without him, the Greeley Gremlins would have little or no chance to win the game against St. Joseph High School, who also had an excellent center. Greeley's back-up center had never played more than three minutes in a game and was a very nervous 6'3" sophomore.

When the tardiness rule was accepted by the faculty last spring, Bob had thought about something like this happening. The policy stated that any athlete who came to school after 10:00 A.M. on the day of a game without a legitimate excuse would not be allowed to play. At 10:08, Billy had told Janet that he was so excited about the game that he had not fallen asleep until 3:30 A.M. and so had overslept. Billy begged Janet to write 9:59 on the sign-in sheet and even though she was the only person in the office at the time, she refused Billy's request. After he had left for class she had called Bob and his response had been to ask Janet for a few minutes to think about what should be done.

Bob recalled that since the policy's inception, four or five student athletes had been denied the right to participate in a game. Thus far, the rule had not caused any of the problems that Bob had predicted during the faculty debate. He was sure that had last year's basketball team been more responsible, there never would have been such a rule. Last year, several team members had the habit of coming in late on game days, so the principal and a number of faculty members pushed for the current policy. When Bob had argued that a student violating the rule should have at least one warning before being punished, a faculty member replied that if a student couldn't get to school by 10:00 A.M., he shouldn't have the privilege of playing that day. Principal Hensel commented that keeping track of warnings would just give his overworked secretary one more thing to do and in the end, a majority of the faculty had voted for the rule.

Bob knew he had very few options. Even if he asked his friend Janet to write 9:59 on the sign-in sheet, such falsification would probably not remain a secret. A second alternative would be to allow Billy to ask one of his parents to write a note saying that he had been sick. He was not sure that he could bring himself to have Billy ask his parents to lie.

It occurred to Bob that he probably should talk to Coach Lindsay about the dilemma. Coach Lindsay had been extremely excited all week and he was the type of coach who had to fight to control himself in tense situations. It was impossible to predict how he would react to the news that his star player could be ineligible for tonight's game. The coach hated the rule and during the faculty debate had pointed out that neither the student council president nor the yearbook editor were disciplined for tardiness. He even angrily noted that a student coming in late on the day of the honor society induction had not been barred from participating in the ceremony that evening. Bob decided not to talk to the coach at this point.

He knew he should discuss the incident with Jim Hensel, the high school principal and it was not too difficult to know how Jim would respond. A typical Hensel reaction would be, "the kid broke the rule, he has to pay the consequences." The athletic director could point out that Billy had not been late since the rule had been put into effect, although it was unfortunately true that Billy was one of the reasons the rule was passed in the first place. In his junior year, he had been one of the boys who had on occasion come in late on game days. This was not because Billy disliked school; he was an above average student and a number of colleges were scouting him. There would certainly be a number of college coaches at the game tonight and there was a distinct possibility he would be offered a number of athletic scholarships.

Bob fully expected that none of this information would affect the principal's judgment. Jim Hensel had articulated one goal with the faculty this year and that was to raise academic achievement as demonstrated by test scores. He had even questioned the need for a pep assembly during school hours. Concerned about losing instructional time and not at all fond of pep assemblies, Jim had initially suggested that the pep assembly be held after school, but in the end, agreed to honor the request of the team and cheerleaders. In any case, there seemed to be little chance that the principal would be flexible in dealing with Billy Lyons.

There were other interested parties, including a very active sports booster club that included over one hundred community members. They were already planning a year-end banquet to honor the basketball team and raising money to buy each of the boys a jacket commemorating their great season. Coach Lindsay was very active with the boosters and he did not hesitate to use the their influence when it could be helpful to his program. Bob also thought about another group who might have their own interpretation of any decision made in this matter. Billy Lyons was the only African-American boy on the team and Bob wondered whether some of the African-American parents would suggest that if it had been Tommy Benson instead of Billy Lyons who had come in late, he would be playing. Tommy, the student council president, was the son of the president of the Board of Education, and although Bob knew that race would not affect Jim Hensel's decision, some parents might find it hard to believe.

Of course, the superintendent, Mary Ellen Baker, would be very sensitive to groups like the sports booster club and the African-American parents, but Bob was not at all sure how she would react to this set of circumstances. While she certainly cared about the community's reaction, she also would be hesitant to not support a policy that had been put in place by a majority of the high school faculty. If the administration did not enforce the rule, a number of teachers would suggest that all they cared about was winning and satisfying the community. Knowing Mary Ellen, Bob imagined her calling a Board of Education meeting and delegating the decision to them. If the high school principal made the decision first, both the superintendent and the board would be hesitant to overrule him. Jim Hensel was a principal who did not appreciate being second-guessed and he would also be upset with Bob if the athletic director chose to go to the superintendent first. It seemed that all of Bob's options were bad, but he had to do something because Janet was waiting in the high school office for him to call her back.

## POSSIBLE DISCUSSION QUESTIONS

1. As Bob attempts to determine a course of action, what factors should be primary in making a decision?

2. What do you think that you would do if you were in the athletic director's position? Why?

*Case Study 9*

# Cutting the Budget

Administrators spend a significant amount of time preparing and defending budget proposals. Although the Board of Education must approve school budgets, it is the department chairpersons, principals, and central office administrators who do most of the preliminary work on the annual budget. In communities where the voting public has the final word, the school budget can become a major political issue. Developing a budget is most difficult when expected revenues will not support even the existing program. When this occurs, school districts are faced with painful decisions. In this case study, the administrative team must submit to the Board of Education a list of cuts which they feel will do the least harm to the educational program of the school district.

Middleport is a less than affluent suburban school district with approximately 2,000 students. It had called for a 3.4 percent property tax increase by a vote of 401 to 388 and there had been significant opposition, in large part because the increase had been higher than the previous year's 1.7 percent increase in the Consumer Price Index. In addition, between four hundred and five hundred blue collar workers had lost their jobs during the twelve months prior to the budget vote. As the school administrators prepared their new budget, an announcement was made that an additional three hundred workers would lose their jobs. They were also aware that the increase during the past year of the Consumer Price Index was again below 2 percent.

In her early thinking about the budget, Superintendent Linda Rensen knew that this was not going to be a year for new staff or new programs, even though the number of students in the district was expected to increase by fifty. At first, she was hopeful that with a decent state aid bill, the district could hold the line on property taxes and maintain its current program, but as she examined the projected state aid figures, this proved to be a false hope. The amount was approximately 4 percent less than they had received this year. Although she and the business official checked and rechecked the figures, the fact was that because of the weak economy, the state government itself had revenue problems and had cut educational aid, along with most other areas in the state budget.

With all of these factors in mind, Linda and her administrative team had prepared an extremely tight draft budget to present to the Board of Education. It proposed increasing property taxes by $600,000, an increase of just under 8 percent. Obviously, the board was unhappy with the proposal. Linda explained that the large property tax increase was due to the major reduction in state aid, and after an hour-and-a-half discussion on the poor economy, a motion requesting that the administration present a prioritized list of cuts in the proposed budget was unanimously passed. These cuts were to total at least $300,000, and were to be presented at the next board meeting. After the motion was passed, one board member suggested that "it would be nice to have more than $300,000 of cuts so that the board would have some latitude in making decisions." This idea was not part of the resolution that was accepted by the board. It was clear to Linda that at this point, not one of the seven board members would support a tax increase of more than 3 percent.

Several days after the board meeting, Linda called together the business administrators and the four building principals and spent several hours coming up with a list of potential cuts. For Linda, it was like pulling teeth. At first, no one in the meeting was willing to put forward suggestions which would hurt their own program. Expecting that this might be the case, Linda had gone into the meeting with her own list. As she introduced each potential cut, there was at least token opposition to all of them. Well into the meeting, the entire group finally began to cooperate in an effort to find those cuts which would be least painful to the school program. Mrs. Simmons, the superintendent's secretary, had taken notes on these suggestions and put together a brief description of each cut. When she finished typing the random list of suggestions, she brought them to the superintendent. Linda was now reading them over in order to decide what to do next.

| **Budget Cut** | **Explanation** |
|---|---|
| 1. $40,000—Cut one second grade teacher. | There will be one retirement of an elementary school teacher at the end of this year. After studying the projected enrollments for next year, it was clear that the only elementary grade level where a position could be cut would be the second grade. Because the district has a provision in its teacher contract that calls for elementary class sizes not to exceed twenty-seven, it is the second grade where a cut could be made. |

The result will be a projected increase in average class size at that level from twenty-two to twenty-six students.

2. $140,000—cut seven teacher aides in the kindergarten.

When kindergarten class size reached twenty-two students per class several years ago, the district created a para-professional teacher aide position for every kindergarten classroom. *partial cut possible.

3. Cuts in the athletic program
   a. $2,200—cuts in elementary intramural program.
   b. $12,500—substitute middle school intramural programs for the four interscholastic programs for boys and girls.

Currently, an after school program is offered for fifth and sixth graders each semester. *partial cut possible.

Such a cut would end the practice of having middle school teams compete against other schools. This would save money on coaches' salaries, transportation costs, and payments to referees. In place of this program, we would substitute several after school coed intramural opportunities for the middle school children.

   c. $6,000—cut the high school wrestling program (twenty-one students and the wrestling cheerleading squad—ten students).
   d. $3,500—cut the tennis program.

Participation in this sport is down from thirty-five students several years ago to twenty-one this year. We were not able to fill all of the weight classes in the junior varsity and varsity teams.

Participation in this sport is also declining. The school has gone from twenty-seven students to seventeen.

4. Extracurricular cuts
   a. $800—cut chess club advisor.
   b. $1,000—cut literary publication advisor.

Only nine students participate in this club.

Only fourteen students were involved in the publication of the literary journal.

5. $24,000—cut night cleaner in the high school building.

With one of the night shift retiring, the remaining four cleaners would have to increase the number of areas they clean each evening. The superintendent of buildings and grounds believes that this would necessitate that some areas not be thoroughly cleaned every day. The school is an 800 student building. *partial cut possible.

6. $25,000—cut one secretary.

Each of the four buildings has two secretaries. The principals argue that this is necessary for the efficient functioning of their offices. This cut, which also becomes possible because of a retirement, would reduce the office of the smallest elementary school to one secretary. This school has an enrollment of 275 students. *partial cut possible.

7. $40,000—cut one secondary social studies teacher.

After completely rescheduling the department faculties in grades 7 through 12, this cut would raise the average class size from twenty-three to twenty-seven. Three social studies teachers would have to take on an extra preparation and one would have to divide his or her time between the high school and middle school. This cut also would not require letting a teacher go, as there will be a retirement in the social studies department. *partial cut possible.

8. $17,000—suspend all district field trips for the coming year.

It is possible that some trips could be paid for by the students or by donations from local civic organizations. *partial cut possible.

9. Raise $4,000 in revenue by charging community groups for using the buildings in the evening.

Currently, community organizations are allowed to use the buildings free of charge.

10. $2,500—cut the school marching band.

We would keep the band but reduce the extra pay that the band director gets for the marching band and also save money on the transportation costs for this group. (Band currently plays at football games, two local parades and two out of town parades.)

11. $1,500—cut the position of part time tax collector.

The business office secretary would take on this role. This would take most of her time during eight weeks in the fall.

12. $24,000—cut summer school reading program.

This program offers remedial reading instruction for approximately eighty elementary students who are below grade level in reading.

13. $24,000—cut study hall monitor position.

This job would be eliminated. An extra study hall would be picked up by secondary department chairpersons. These individuals are responsible for developing schedules and budgets, along with helping new teachers. They do not do classroom observations. This cut would give them only two periods free in an eight-period day, rather than three. It should be noted that these teachers are compensated an additional $1,500 per year for their duties as department chairpersons.

14. $21,000—cut in supplies, equipment and textbooks.

Last year, the district spent $520,000 in these combined areas. Teachers had been disappointed in this amount. If this cut is accepted, there would be a 4 percent reduction in what would be spent in the coming year. *partial cut possible.

15. $6,000—cut student custodial help during the summer.

This item in the budget allowed the district to employ six students to work with the custodial and maintenance staff crews during the summer.

As Linda studied the list, she was grateful that it did not require laying off any professional personnel, and only the study hall monitor position was being eliminated from the nonteaching staff. Still, she knew that if there had been sufficient revenues, she would not have recommended any of these cuts. After Linda dictated a memo to the business official and four principals requesting their prioritized lists of cuts, she began to prioritize her own.

## POSSIBLE DISCUSSION QUESTIONS

1. Prioritize the cuts you would recommend to the Board of Education. The total should come to $300,000. Where noted, partial cuts can be made, but you should explain how such a cut would be implemented.

2. Should the superintendent ask for the administrative list in writing and then use them as advisory data in preparing her final list to the board? Or would you as superintendent call another meeting for additional discussion with the hope that some sort of consensus could be reached within the administrative team?

3. Should the superintendent present a list to the board of more than $300,000 of prioritized cuts? Would it be better to hold back any additional cuts in case they were demanded at the meeting?

4. Are there other areas in any school budget that you think an administrative team should consider for cuts?

5. Should the superintendent seek to have the Board of Education raise their 3 percent capital on a tax increase?

6. What, if any, problems are caused when the public defeats a budget proposal?

## Case Study 10

# The Music Lesson Dilemma

With the recent pressure on schools to raise academic achievement, teachers are increasingly defensive about students missing class for any reason. In this case study, the issue involves allowing students to be released from class for instrumental music lessons. Many schools use a rotating schedule to allow instrumental music teachers to meet with various sections of the band or orchestra for group lessons. Instrumental music teachers have long maintained that large ensemble rehearsals are not enough to develop an adequate band or orchestra and that these lessons are necessary if students are to improve their skills. In many communities, parents cannot or will not pay for private lessons outside of school. This case study presents the conflict between the chair of the music department, who defends release time lessons, and a group of academic teachers, who want their students in class every day.

Sharon Roberts, a second-year high school principal, was beginning to question the wisdom of starting her high school advisory council. She had envisioned the group as a principal's cabinet, advising her on various issues facing the high school. Having learned in her college administration courses about the advantages of participatory management, she had decided to try out the theory. Elected by the entire faculty, the group of seven teachers had now been meeting for several months. Sharon decided at their second meeting to raise the issue of academic test scores in the district. In comparison with other area schools, Eden Central's test results were, at best, mediocre. After the last results were published, the Board of Education made it clear to the administration that raising these student test scores should be the district's primary objective during the coming year.

While the council considered ways to improve the test results, one of the English teachers remarked that a major problem was that students were too often absent from class. No one on the council disagreed with this comment. Mr. Finch, a European history teacher, added that it seemed like his students were out of class for instrumental music lessons every other week. Mrs. Lemm, the chairperson of the science department, agreed, noting that she had calculated that instrumental students had missed her chemistry classes and labs at least ten times during the last year. As the discussion continued, someone pointed out that the lessons were rotated during six periods, and therefore, every six weeks the students would miss a particular class. In addition, the band did a short tour each year and missed several other classes. Mr. Finch commented that if the council was really serious about improving test scores, music lessons during class time should be terminated. "Let them take their lesson during their free period or after school," he said. Everyone on the council agreed that release time lessons were a problem. As a next step, a motion was made and seconded that the chairperson of the music department, who was also the band director, be invited to the next meeting. Before Sharon even thought very much about the motion, it had been unanimously approved by the group.

The principal knew that it was her job to issue the invitation. Frank Costello had been in charge of instrumental music in the school for twenty-three years. The music program was his life and he was extremely proud of his student musicians. The band had won numerous awards in area competitions and graduates frequently returned to see their former conductor and to sit in on rehearsals. More than a dozen of his students had gone on to become music teachers or professional musicians. Strongly committed to the music program, Frank seldom socialized with other teachers and some joked that in twenty-three years, Frank had never even seen the faculty. If you wanted to talk with him, you had to go to the music area where you could find him from 7:00 A.M. until 5:30 P.M., every day.

Despite his self-imposed isolation, Frank was quick to sense danger. When Sharon invited him to attend the meeting, he immediately became excited and defensive about the music program. According to Frank, "they were out to destroy the best thing we have going in this school. Our band has put Eden on the map. Without these lessons and only three rehearsals a week, the program would crumble."

When Sharon tried to calm Frank down, he only became more agitated and said, "I'll go to the superintendent, I'll go to the Board of Education, I'll go to the commissioner, I'll go to the Pope. Sharon, you can't do this to me. It will ruin everything I've worked for." This was the longest speech that Sharon had ever heard from Frank and there was no question about the depth of his feeling. Suddenly, the council meeting scheduled for tomorrow didn't seem like a very good idea.

As principal and chairperson of the council, it would be her job to maintain order and ensure civility during the meeting. As she thought about the possible outcome, she was uncertain of how the inevitable conflict would be resolved. Of course, it was possible that Frank's emotional appeal would change the minds of the faculty. If he had only been more popular, the academic teachers would probably be more likely to compromise. As it was, Sharon could not see Mr. Finch and Mrs. Lemm modifying their positions. Besides, Sharon wasn't sure she could support the students missing six or seven classes per year.

In her conversation with Frank, the principal had explored the idea of finding a compromise. She suggested taking the students out of their study halls for lessons. Frank had explained to her that this would make it impossible to have a sectional lesson. Scheduling all of the trumpet players in grades nine through twelve for the same study hall just could not be done. What he would end up with would be a sectional rehearsal with two flutes, a tuba, a bass drum, and an oboe. Frank said emphatically, "It just wouldn't work." Sharon suggested that lessons could be given after school, but that too seemed unworkable. She even suggested that Frank come to school at 10:30 A.M. and have his sectional rehearsals from 2:30 to 5:00. To this alternative, Frank pointed out that a large number of his students were athletes. He asked, "Do you think the coaches are going to allow students to miss practice to play their horns?" By the end of the meeting with Frank, Sharon had been able to find no acceptable compromise.

Not only did Sharon have no clear plan for the meeting, she had no clear picture as to how a final decision would be made. Should she vote on the issue at the council meeting? If the council maintained its position that release time lessons should end, should she have the entire faculty vote on the proposal? Since this group's role was only to advise, was the decision really hers alone? Sharon wished that she had thought a little more carefully about the concept of participatory democracy.

## POSSIBLE DISCUSSION QUESTIONS

1. What should be the principal's plan for the upcoming meeting?

2. Should she say at the outset of the meeting that she realized the final decision was hers, but that she wanted to hear from both sides?

3. Should Sharon take a vote of the council after the discussion?

4. Should the entire faculty debate and vote on this issue?

5. Would it be wise for her to speak with the superintendent about the issue?

6. Can you think of any type of compromise to resolve this conflict?

7. What would be your overall administrative strategy in this situation?

# The Tenure Decision

One of the most important decisions an administrator must make is whether a teacher should be recommended for tenure. Although terminating a probationary teacher is relatively easy, dismissing a tenured professional can be a long and expensive process. A school district should have in place an effective and fair plan for supervision and evaluation of faculty members. Sometimes, even when a teacher is carefully supervised, the decision can be difficult.

Dr. Ruth Kinney was still disturbed after her conversation with the high school principal, Peter Gonzalez. Ruth had been a superintendent for seven years and had never failed to recommend a third-year probationary teacher for tenure. It had been her policy to make a decision on a teacher by the end of the second year. She felt that carrying someone for three years was unnecessary and if teachers could not prove themselves in two years, they probably were not right for permanent employment in the district. Now, her high school principal had told her in no uncertain terms that James Oswald should not be granted tenure.

During their conversation, Peter said that he had "tried everything with the man, but nothing had solved the problem." Ruth remembered reading both of Mr. Oswald's annual evaluation reports and they contained many positive comments about his creative teaching and involvement in extra-curricular activities. His Model United Nations Club had hosted two large regional conferences and these weekend meetings had brought favorable attention to the school district. Ruth herself had attended the sessions and found them well organized and effective. Those parents who had watched the debates commented favorably on the event and the local newspaper had even written an editorial complementing Mr. Oswald and the school. There was no question that he was popular with the students and had made many friends in the community, including membership in the local Kiwanis Club. Ruth also remembered that significant portions of Mr. Oswald's evaluations were devoted to suggesting ways to improve his writing skills.

Specifically, there was a note both years on spelling errors that had been made during lessons, on reports and in communications with parents.

In reviewing the situation with Ruth, Peter had enumerated the steps he had taken to deal with the problem. During his first year, when it became obvious that Mr. Oswald was misspelling words in the comments section of report cards as well as in progress reports to parents, Peter began to check Mr. Oswald's documents before they were sent out. Even with this kind of censorship, parents continued to bring Peter examples of notes with misspelled words that Mr. Oswald had written on homework papers and tests. When observing his class, the principal noted that Mr. Oswald had misspelled words on the blackboard during his lessons and there was even a sign hanging in the room with a misspelled word. Students often corrected his spelling and some of his errors brought giggles from the sophomores. Peter had strongly recommended that Mr. Oswald make overheads and refrain from writing spontaneously on the board. He was instructed to allow Janet Baker, the department chair, to check any overhead transparencies he planned to use during his lessons. While he continued to have some problems during the spring semester of his second year, there seemed to be fewer reports of poor grammar and spelling. Although torn with doubt, Peter had decided not to recommend dismissal after the second year because he thought that the problem was solvable.

Unfortunately, the third year of the probationary period had been even worse than the second, and now the principal was angry. He had concluded that the teacher couldn't or wouldn't change. Peter had commented to the superintendent, "The man must have Attention Deficit Disorder. I don't see him ever sitting still long enough to write a literate paragraph. You should see what his comments on students' yearbooks look like. There is no question in my mind that he has a serious learning disability. Believe me, I've tried everything. Even with constant monitoring, he will continue to embarrass us. Many parents know about the problem and brought it to my attention. I would be very surprised if a member of the Board of Education doesn't ask about it before they vote on his tenure."

Ruth asked Peter how they had missed the problem when they hired Mr. Oswald. Peter noted that his college references were exceptional, and although one college supervisor gave him unfavorable marks in language arts skills, none of his references mentioned his spelling problem. He had been a member of the student senate, president of the Future Teachers Club, and his grade point average was almost a B. There was no way the problem could have been determined from his records.

While there was no question in Ruth's mind about Peter's recommendation, she knew not recommending tenure would be met with opposition. Even though Peter had documented many of Mr. Oswald's spelling and grammar errors, she did not doubt that the faculty union would support the teacher. She also knew that most of his students, past and present, would denounce the administration for not recommending tenure. The community itself would be split, but Mr. Oswald had made enough friends that there would be major opposition to a decision not to grant tenure. Most of all, she was worried about the Board of Education. How would they react to a public controversy? She had not yet been through a major conflict with the board and didn't wish this to be the first. It was also true that she had always been supportive of her building principals in the past and did not wish to lose their trust.

Between now and the Board of Education meeting next Thursday, Ruth would have to decide on whether or not to recommend tenure for Mr. Oswald. Like so many decisions, this seemed to be one that could only cause her new problems.

## POSSIBLE DISCUSSION QUESTIONS

1. What, if anything, could Ruth do to help make her decision for the upcoming meeting?

2. If you were an assistant superintendent in the district and the superintendent asked for advice on this issue, what would you suggest?

3. If she decides not to recommend tenure, what should Ruth emphasize in her presentation to the board?

4. If she decides to recommend tenure, what can she say to Peter Gonzalez and the other principals?

5. If the teacher leaves the district and asks for a recommendation, how should Ruth respond?

6. What, if anything, can Ruth do to try to avoid this type of problem in the future?

## Case Study 12

# Loyalty

Like any organization, school districts are likely to experience times when individuals or groups are heavily engaged in power struggles. Such a conflict can engulf an entire administrative team and sometimes the stakes can be high, not only for the school district, but for the individuals involved. Even if they are not personally engaged in the dispute, middle level administrators can be drawn into the struggle. At a time like this, the administrator must decide where his or her loyalties should lie.

Rick Coleman, the assistant superintendent for curriculum and personnel, was busy setting up interviews for the fourteen teaching positions which were open in the district. During recent months, he had worked hard to concentrate on his job, even though he was well aware that his boss, Superintendent Gary Leesman, was engaged in an ongoing battle with three members of the Board of Education. For over a year, there had been numerous four-to-three votes on issues supported by the superintendent. On several occasions, there had been frequent exchanges at public Board of Education meetings, and some of the comments had been quoted in the local newspaper. As a result of this conflict, board member Florence Johnson, a detractor of the superintendent, had become active in the Board of Education election and had openly supported the candidacy of the incumbent, Keith Emerson, a strong supporter of the superintendent. Keith had narrowly won the election, and although he had never commented publicly that he favored dismissing the superintendent, it was widely believed that, influenced by Florence, he had now come to that conclusion.

Rick's previous boss, Rita March, had also been a controversial superintendent and had become engaged in a political struggle with the Board of Education. Several of the current board members had been heavily involved in the conflict that ended in Rita's dismissal. Although it cost the district almost $100,000, the board had voted to buy out her contract, which gave them the opportunity to choose a new superintendent. After interviewing many candidates, including several from within the district, the board had unanimously chosen Gary Leesman. Gary apparently had had a successful tenure in a small neighboring community, and on coming to the district, he had been given a five-year contract by the board.

After his "honeymoon period," Gary began to slowly make enemies within the district. A former English teacher, his written work was clear and concise, and although he was an articulate public speaker, he was extremely reserved in small groups. Unfortunately, Gary seldom smiled and didn't really enjoy "small talk" or most social occasions. As he began to hear criticism of himself, the superintendent became increasingly isolated and spent his days in his office dictating memos and letters to people in the district. Although Gary's correspondence was well written, many recipients thought it similar to that of a military commander. One principal had compared him to Richard Nixon in the final days before his resignation. His infrequent administrative meetings were primarily a monologue, and at Board of Education meetings he appeared to be offended when his recommendations were questioned. These public sessions had become increasingly tense as individual members became more obvious in their disrespect for the superintendent.

Rick Coleman continued to get along well with the board members, but when he was ordered by the superintendent to give a presentation supporting an unpopular program, several of the members had become short with him as well. His wife, Kelly, had commented on how unlike himself Rick had become before and after the meetings. Usually not prone to worry about such matters, he had come to dread these public sessions. In recent informal conversations with other administrators, it seemed clear to Rick that nearly all of them would be glad to see the superintendent relieved of his duty.

With the exception of the elementary principal, the superintendent had no personal friends in the district, and even though Rick should have been Gary's chief adviser, they had never become close. The two top administrators in the district did not even call each other by their first names and frequently would go days without speaking to each other. That is not to say that Gary did not make his will known in written communication. As the assistant superintendent, Rick received as many as three memos a day ordering him to take some kind of action, including reprimanding and on occasion dismissing certain staff members. When Rick objected to an order, he had to make an appointment to see his boss and although Gary would listen, only occasionally would he modify his orders. Despite the fact that he did not approve of the superintendent's management style, Rick had learned to live with it and do his job. For the most part, he had managed to stay out of the line of fire between the beleaguered superintendent and his critics.

Last evening, Florence Johnson had called him at home and there was now a major effort to draw Rick into the struggle. Usually he could joke with Florence and manage to avoid being embroiled in the politics of the district, but this time, she was determined to force Rick to respond. She made it clear that the board was going to fire Gary using a clause in his contract that stated he could be dismissed for "incompetence." She went on to say that the board majority "had put together an overwhelming case" which would be persuasive even if Gary attempted to dispute it in court. When Rick asked for examples, she replied that the superintendent had neglected to do required written evaluations of administrative personnel. Rick knew that he had been evaluated during Gary's first year, but this year the procedure was not yet completed and the superintendent had missed the deadline. Florence also said that the 15 percent tax increase that the superintendent had recommended in the draft of the budget this year demonstrated his incompetence. The board had asked for a "zero-base budget" and had instead been given a 15 percent tax increase proposal. Most important, she reported to Rick, was that "numerous administrators, faculty, and staff had shared with board members accounts of the superintendent's incompetence." When Rick inquired who these individuals were, Florence replied that "this information is confidential at this time." Before their conversation ended, Florence had told Rick that she would stop by his house on Saturday morning to pick up his accounts demonstrating the superintendent's incompetence. When Rick suggested that he wasn't sure that he wanted to do this, Florence made clear that "it would be a good idea for you to cooperate." Tomorrow morning, Florence would be on his doorstep and Rick had made a list of those things that bothered him about the superintendent.

1. Primarily, he was disturbed about his boss's cold and impersonal style and the fact that he almost never praised anyone for the good work they had done.
2. He was not a good listener and his decisions were seldom affected by the opinions of others.
3. He delegated all of the unpleasant tasks to his subordinates.
4. If the subordinate was in trouble, Gary often did not support that individual.
5. On several occasions, the superintendent had publicly criticized Rick in the presence of other professional staff members.
6. He attempted to take credit for all of the successes in the district and none of the problems.
7. He had created a stressful and unhappy working environment in the district central office.

On the other hand, Rick was not aware that the superintendent had ever done anything that was either illegal or unethical; Gary's personal habits and morals appeared to be above reproach, his knowledge of education law, finance, and curriculum was extensive and it seemed to Rick that among his fellow superintendents, Gary had earned a high level of respect.

As Rick pondered his position with the board, he asked himself what was meant by the term "professional incompetence." A more immediate question was what, if anything, he should say to Florence in the meeting. Where should his loyalty lie? Should it be with the boss who he dislikes or with the critical and angry

Board members who seek to dismiss him?

## POSSIBLE DISCUSSION QUESTIONS

1. As a "middle manager," what level of loyalty do you owe to your superintendent?

2. At what point, if ever, does a "middle manager" participate in an effort to dismiss his supervisor in an organization?

3. What would you say to the board members if you were in Rick's position?

## Case Study 13

# Who Should Sing in the School Chorus?

Performing music groups can reflect positively on the school that they represent, and music teachers obviously feel that the performance level of these groups also illustrates their own competence. One of the great satisfactions of their profession is to receive a positive audience response at concerts. At the same time, the school chorus should be considered an integral part of the music education curriculum and it can be argued that the experience of performing in a musical group should be open to as many students as possible. This case study illustrates the conflict between those seeking broad participation and those desiring high quality performances.

Mary Quinn was a brand new music teacher at John Hunt Elementary School. She was twenty-two years old, enthusiastic, and very idealistic. Only a week into her first year of teaching, she was now having a difference of opinion with the district music coordinator, Ron Hargrove, which she had just shared with her principal, Sylvia Kinsey.

The young teacher had gone into Sylvia's office to announce her disagreement with a music department policy that she felt was absolutely wrong and should be changed immediately. Although it took a while, Sylvia was finally able to get Mary to identify the terrible problem. It seemed that for the past nineteen years, her predecessor in the elementary music position had conducted auditions for the elementary chorus. Selecting only the forty most talented students for the John Hunt Elementary School Chorus, he had developed a performing group which was greatly admired in the community. Along with their three well-attended concerts each year, the chorus sang at the senior citizen's center, nursing homes, and other schools. They had even performed several times with the local symphony orchestra. Mary, however, did not believe in auditions at the elementary school level. She was committed to the idea that any child who wanted to participate should be allowed to join the group. Her chorus sign-up had ninety-six students from grades 4 through 6 and Mary felt that no one should be denied the opportunity to sing. When Sylvia suggested she might have twenty-five children who could not even carry a tune, Mary had replied, "I can live with that." Sylvia had also asked her how she expected to maintain order and discipline with that many students, especially since some of the children had just signed up to get out of their homeroom for a couple of hours a week. Once again, Mary was confident that her rehearsals would be so well planned that the students wouldn't have time to misbehave. She also noted that during her student teaching, she had worked with a large chorus without any serious problems. Before leaving Sylvia's office, Mary made a final plea that she just be allowed to try it her way.

Sylvia knew that the music coordinator, Ron Hargrove, would not be sympathetic to Mary's plan, since he had always taken great pride in the quality of the John Hunt Elementary Chorus. It was perhaps the most successful performing group in the school district and Ron had always traveled to their programs and personally introduced the group to the audience. For him, the John Hunt Elementary Chorus was extremely helpful in projecting a positive image for the music department. At a time when music was considered by many district residents as a "frill" Ron had used it to entertain and bring pleasure to the community. By only including students with musical ability, the group had become a truly outstanding ensemble, and Ron would undoubtedly argue that the quality of the music would be lost if the school opened the chorus to all children.

To add to the problem, Ron had not favored hiring Mary Quinn as music teacher. He would have preferred to have another candidate with eleven years experience and who he was convinced could maintain the tradition of excellence that the chorus had established. Sylvia had thought the experienced candidate rather ordinary whereas Mary Quinn had the energy, intelligence, and commitment which would guarantee her success in the classroom. Even though it had been obvious that she was a bit naive, her willingness to work hard and her sparkling personality would undoubtedly make her a favorite with the children. It had now become obvious in her first week that Mary was not shy and could be a bit stubborn; she certainly was not acting like the typical first-year teacher. In any case, Sylvia had taken a strong position on hiring Mary and the superintendent had followed her recommendation, but now, Mary was about to upset the man who had not wanted to hire her in the first place. Sylvia could have told Mary that this was not the time to change the old policy and that maybe in a few years the school could expand the elementary chorus. As principal, she could tell Mary that she was to have auditions.

Yet Sylvia did not totally disagree with Mary's position on the matter. Maybe in the high school there was a place for competition and tryouts, but she, too, disliked excluding children at the elementary school level. Perhaps she should just go to the music coordinator and suggest that they give Mary a chance to try it her way. Sylvia had almost decided on this course of action when it occurred to her that the venerable superintendent, Dr. Baird, was also a great fan of the John Hunt Elementary Chorus. A rather serious musician, he would be the first to notice if the quality of the chorus declined. Sylvia could not help but think how complicated even a seemingly simple decision could become.

## POSSIBLE DISCUSSION QUESTIONS

1. Do you think that an elementary chorus should be open to all children?

2. How would you deal with this issue if you were the elementary school principal?

*Case Study 14*

# The Bond Issue

Most educational administrators become involved in efforts to gain public support for building or renovation projects. As schools age and fall into disrepair, and increased enrollments place added pressure on existing facilities, these initiatives become crucial. Since they are financed in large part by local property taxes, it is often difficult to gain public support for such projects.

In many districts, two-thirds of the eligible voters do not have children enrolled in public schools. There are younger voters who have not yet become parents of school-aged children and parents whose children have recently graduated. The fastest growing group is the retired citizen who is often living on a fixed income. Each of these voter groups must be convinced that borrowing money to improve schools is a good investment. Planning such a campaign is usually not covered in college courses and there are not many opportunities to get it right. The purpose of this case study is to challenge the reader to develop a strategy that will ensure a positive vote for a proposed bond issue.

It was an inauspicious beginning. After almost two hours of vigorous debate, the Board of Education had voted five to two to hold a referendum on a building bond issue. At the urging of Superintendent John Forsythe, a school district facilities committee had been formed to create a plan for meeting the future needs of the district. The fifteen-member committee consisted of a cross section of district citizens, faculty and several administrators. John had chaired the group and was quite satisfied with the consensus that had emerged as a result of their year-long efforts. He was certain that all of the committee members would actively support the plan.

The group had done their work carefully, taking advantage of the services of architects, engineers, and a school financial consultant. John was relieved when the board voted to put the proposal on the ballot, because the committee had spent almost $10,000 in professional fees in preparing the report. In its final form, the recommendations called for a bond issue totaling $11.5 million.

The morning after the board meeting, John made a list of those facts that he felt might be crucial in developing a public campaign for support of the building project:

1. The entire $11.5 million would be financed by the sale of bonds prior to beginning the project.
2. Although the district was borrowing this amount, they would be paying out a similar amount in interest payments during the twenty-five-year life of the bond issue. In reality, the building project would cost over $20 million.
3. During those twenty-five years, the district would be receiving state aid each year to pay approximately 80 percent of the principal and interest costs for the project.
4. Because the building project would take two years and payment to the contractors and architects would be spaced out over that time period, the district would be able to earn interest during the construction period. That money could be used during the first two years of payment to reduce the local share of the cost.
5. Although it was difficult to know the exact impact on property taxpayers, the financial consultant estimated that a resident paying $1,000 a year in property tax would pay an additional $30 to $40 a year in taxes to pay for the building project, although larger taxpayers would pay much more.
6. For this money, the district would be able to build a middle school addition on the east side of the current one-story building. Along with major alterations, a new middle school for grades 5–8 could be established. By moving the fifth and sixth grades to this new building, the elementary school could then comfortably house grades K–4. The project called for the middle school addition to include a new library, gymnasium, office, conference room, and remodeled music and art areas. Because grades 9–12 would be giving up classrooms to the middle school, a four-room addition would be built on the west side of the building for high school classrooms. Finally, the plan presented to the board called for major work on the school campus, including a fenced-in girls' softball field and new tennis courts. New trees, bushes, and lighting, along with repairing the parking area, were also part of the plan.
7. In defending the need for these projects, the committee report had emphasized the following factors:
   a. The current elementary facilities were already overcrowded. Music, art, and remedial reading teachers were without their own classrooms. A windowless closet storeroom was being used to house four desks for faculty members who had no rooms. The speech therapist was working in a converted custodial storeroom, and because there was no place

assigned to the instrumental music teacher, her lessons were given in
the school cafeteria.

b. In the 7–12 building, nine teachers were without classrooms of their
own and taught their classes in rooms where the regular teacher had a
planning period. These traveling teachers were assigned desks in two
converted closet areas and it was difficult for them to find a quiet place
to meet with students for conversation or tutoring. Even the teachers
who had their own classrooms had to vacate them during their free periods. With no classrooms available for study halls, over one hundred
students were assigned to the cafeteria each period. Even though teachers were assigned to this large study hall, it was extremely difficult to
maintain an atmosphere conducive to quiet study.

8. Student census figures showed that the kindergarten enrollment would
grow in each of the next four years. Without providing new classroom
areas, the overcrowding would only become worse.

9. The outside appearance of the secondary school was barren and stark and
aesthetically unpleasing. Neither the tennis courts nor the parking lots had
been paved for many years. The proposed additional lighting would
improve the appearance of the building at night, as well as offer additional security for the campus. Although the girls' softball team was popular, it lacked a proper field for home games. The boys' baseball team
already had an excellent fenced-in field.

10. The education organization literature strongly supported the middle school
model over the traditional junior high grades 7–9 or the grade 7–12 organization pattern. There seemed to be many persuasive arguments for plac-
ing eleven-to-fourteen-year-olds in a separate environment. These young
people had unique characteristics that called for special programs and
styles of teaching, and it was important to separate them from the negative
influence of some of the older adolescents. A separate cafeteria, library,
and lavatory would help to make this possible. By establishing a separate
organization with its own faculty and principal, this new school could have
its own identity. Research also seemed to demonstrate that smaller schools
could be more effective. The children could have their own newspaper,
yearbook, and student council, and teachers could be trained to treat these
younger children as students in transition, rather than as miniature high
school students.

These arguments had convinced five of the seven board members that the bond
issue vote was needed. The two dissenting members had also made some important points during the debate. John had made notes on their concerns about the
bond issue, as he knew they would come up again during the campaign:

1. The amount of interest we will pay for this project will be exorbitant. Can't we do these projects gradually on a "pay as you go basis"? Why should we pay $11 million in interest costs to wealthy bondholders?

2. Even though growth in enrollment is predicted for the next four years, what assurance do we have that this pattern will not be reversed in the near future? We did see reduced enrollment in the late '70s and '80s and we even closed one school because it was no longer needed. How can we be sure that this will not happen again and we will be paying for classrooms that we don't really need?

3. Is having a classroom for every teacher really that important? Can you prove that this lack of space is in any way affecting student academic achievement?

4. Although everyone would like to improve the appearance of our campus, we must remember that any school tax increase will be difficult for many of our citizens. This district has a high percentage of senior citizens on fixed incomes. Some of these people have already had to give up their homes, in part because of high taxes and even $30 a year will create additional pressure on personal budgets that are already stretched to the limit. In any case, total property tax increases during the next twenty years will be considerably more than $30 a year. During the past fifteen years, school taxes have gone up an average of 5 percent a year, but increases in residents' personal incomes did not come close to that figure. Although many incomes have been stagnant in recent years, most voters know that the salaries of school administrators and teachers have been increasing dramatically. Many citizens believe that their school taxes are already too high.

5. As far as the middle school idea is concerned, where is the evidence that test scores will go up because we have a middle school? Is this just another educational fad like the "new math" that educators claimed would revolutionize our schools?

6. Tennis courts and softball fields are nice to have and we agree that some community members can also benefit from them. People in this community, however, are too busy making a living to have time to be out playing tennis and the people most often seen on the old tennis court are the superintendent and his friends. Do we really need a fenced-in softball field for the girls to have fun playing ball? Can the community afford these luxuries?

John knew that these and other objections were sure to be raised, and although the board had agreed to schedule a bond issue vote, they had not yet committed to the specific aspects of the project. He would try to get their endorsement of all of the elements in the recommendations of the committee. It was his hope that the five members who had voted for the bond issue would consistently support all phases of the project. Whatever the final make-up of the proposal, John knew it would fall upon him to devise a plan for gaining community support.

## POSSIBLE DISCUSSION QUESTIONS

1. Should John and the majority of board members supporting the project compromise on the items to be included in the bond issue in an effort to gain a positive vote of the two individuals who had voted "no"?

2. Assuming that the committee's recommendations are accepted by the board, list the major themes that might be used in the campaign to gain community support.

3. Frame a possible response to each of the objections which were raised by the critics of the report.

4. Write a draft of a short article you would include in the school district newsletter announcing the upcoming bond issue.

*Case Study 15*

# Let's Not Call It Affirmative Action

Recruiting minority members to a school district is a frequent challenge and can become an important issue in urban districts that have a high percentage of minority students. In the present political environment, the term "affirmative action" has a negative connotation for many Americans. Given this reality, many urban administrators, board members, and parents are anxious to include on their faculties as many minority teachers as possible. Today, Caucasians, especially Caucasian males, are extremely sensitive to any plan that they consider discriminatory. Increasingly, women and other minorities also have reservations about initiatives that are referred to as affirmative action programs. In this case study, a new assistant superintendent of schools in an urban setting has been assigned the task of hiring more minority teachers.

Marc Lauzon had only been in his job two weeks when he was given the assignment. As assistant superintendent for personnel, he was responsible for the selection of new teaching and nonteaching employees for the district. In his previous position as a building principal, Marc had been involved in hiring decisions, but the central office had handled the recruitment and initial screening of candidates.

He thought back on his conversation with Superintendent Dan Growell on his third day in his new job. Dan shared with him some data that Marc had found very disturbing. The superintendent pointed out to Marc that in 1960, only 3 percent of the faculty were of a racial minority. With new laws resulting from the civil rights movement, the school district had established an aggressive affirmative action program that included creating goals and quotas for minority faculty. The percentage of minority teachers had gone from 3 percent in 1960 to 29 percent in 1988. What disturbed the superintendent was that since 1988, the percentage of minority faculty had dropped steadily, and by 1998, it was below 20 percent. However, the percentage of minority students in the school system during this period had more than tripled, from 18 percent in 1960 to 65 percent in 1998. Although these figures were not widely known, the superintendent knew that the local chapters of the Urban League and the NAACP were extremely interested in raising the percentage of minority teachers in the district.

As a result of these facts, the superintendent had asked Marc to give some thought to ways that more minority teachers could be hired during the next decade. He was adamant when he said:

> We must change the direction of the way we are moving. I want you to come back in a couple of weeks with some specific ideas on how we should do this. Please don't talk about this issue with anyone except me. Let's not call it affirmative action, but merely a list of strategies we can use to improve our ratio of minority faculty. It is important that we think about this over an extended period, but we also need to find ways to do something next year. When I suggest that you not talk to others about this, I would include the members of the Board of Education. There are several of them who would be very sensitive to this issue.

Marc knew that this assignment was important to his boss and that this would be his first test as the new assistant superintendent for personnel. He wanted to do well, but was nervous about working on a project that might thrust him into city politics. Since being given the assignment, he had done a good deal of reading about the subject and had jotted down some ideas from his readings. Thus far, he really had only created a list of questions.

1. What type of recruiting process might be most effective in meeting the superintendent's assigned goal?
2. Who will make the final decision on hiring new teachers?
3. Can race be considered a factor in making important decisions?
4. How can the district avoid charges of favoritism toward minority teachers?
5. Was the superintendent creating a strategy that would create major problems within the district?
6. Was it possible to implement any plan if its existence was only known to a few key administrators?

As Marc pondered these questions, he knew he needed to conceptualize some ideas for his meeting with the superintendent. He had set aside an hour on the superintendent's calendar in two days time to discuss the issue and he had to come up with something.

## POSSIBLE DISCUSSION QUESTIONS

1. Is this issue one that many districts need to worry about?

2. What should the assistant superintendent suggest to the superintendent in their upcoming meeting?

# Case Study 16

# Is This Child Right for Inclusion?

Since the passage of Public Law 94-142, children determined to be in need of special education have presented many new challenges to school administrators. Initially, most special needs students were taken out of regular classrooms and placed in self-contained programs, and many of these classrooms were used for all categories of special education students. In almost every state, pressure mounted from parents and educators to "mainstream" special education students into regular classrooms, and during the last decade, many schools have gone from resource rooms to full integration of regular classrooms with both learning disabled students and children with more severe problems. As part of this "inclusion," special education teachers have been assigned to regular classrooms to help children in these challenging settings. Although parents, government officials, and college educators have been supportive of the practice of inclusion for social, as well as educational reasons, there is little definitive evidence that these students learn better in a regular classroom, and mainstreaming has become a major political issue in many school districts.

Superintendent Bill Whitney could feel one of his tension headaches coming on. He had listened to the school psychologist Linda Nelson for the past twenty minutes and had been taking notes. It was clear that she was asking for his help on an issue that could have an impact on the entire district.

Linda had worked as a psychologist in the district for almost twenty years and had earned the respect of parents and faculty members. Besides being intelligent and articulate, she was able to communicate effectively and spoke without resorting to the jargon of her profession. She had made hundreds of recommendations to the Committee on Special Education and Linda took pride in the fact that the district had never had to resort to an independent hearing officer to settle a special education conflict. As a diplomat, Linda was skilled in resolving potential problems between parents and the school district. This was the first time she had ever come to the superintendent about a case. Linda had prefaced her comments by saying that because the superintendent was not a member of the Special Education Committee or a voting member of the Board of Education, it was not inappropriate to speak with him prior to the upcoming committee meeting. At this meeting, the group was scheduled to discuss the educational placement of Charlie White for the next year. After retesting and observing Charlie and meeting with his parents, Linda was preparing her formal recommendation to the committee.

Before Linda left his office, Bill had asked for a day to think over the problem. As he began to read through his notes, it was clear the question was whether or not this child was right for inclusion.

## CHARLIE WHITE

1. Age 10.
2. Shorter and smaller than other 10-year-olds.
3. IQ—87.
4. Parents' occupations:
    a. Father is a truck driver who is away from home often.
    b. Mother works as an aide in the school cafeteria.
5. Placed in a special education class after kindergarten. Charlie is currently in a self-contained class with six students, a special education teacher and one aide.
6. While observing Charlie in his classroom, Linda had noted the following behaviors:
    a. He did not sit in his chair for more than three minutes at a time.
    b. He spoke out constantly, interrupting classroom discussion.
    c. He did not appear to be violent or a threat to others, but he did frequently take other students' materials and often angered his classmates.
    d. Although he was not disrespectful, most of the behavior management techniques used by the teacher were ineffective.
    e. He was a disruptive factor in his special education classroom.
7. His parents refuse to take him to a medical specialist for diagnosis. Both the family psychiatrist and Mr. and Mrs. White are opposed to considering any form of drug therapy.
8. Mr. and Mrs. White noted in their meeting with the psychologist that they knew several other special education students had been brought back into the regular classroom and that this is what they want for Charlie. They feel that he needs to get away from those "retarded kids" and be with normal children.
9. Specifically, the parents want their son to be placed in Mrs. Hensen's fourth grade class. Mrs. Hensen is a "wonderful lady." She met Charlie one day at church and knew just how to handle him.

10. Mrs. Hensen told Linda that she would prefer not to have Charlie in her class. She noted that she already had several students diagnosed with Attention Deficit Disorder. In regard to her relationship with Charlie, Mrs. Hensen reported that she only spent five minutes with him one day and certainly had no magic formula for dealing with him.

11. Mrs. Hensen is an experienced and effective teacher, but has had no specific training for dealing with students like Charlie.

12. The Whites have approached an advocate for special education parents and she will be at the next meeting at which Charlie's case will be discussed. In addition to the advocate, an attorney representing the Parent Advocate Organization will be present. It is clear that if the Whites do not get their way at the meeting they will seek an independent hearing officer to hear the case. Linda believes that if this occurs, the school district should retain an attorney to represent the committee and the Board of Education. This could be a costly procedure for the school district.

13. Both the psychologist and Charlie's special education teacher believe it is unlikely that Charlie will succeed in a regular classroom and that he is likely to become disruptive in any classroom setting.

14. In recent months, there have been several complaints by faculty members that special education students had been "dumped" into their classrooms. Although the district has sponsored numerous workshops to help them adjust to "inclusion," most faculty members feel unprepared when severely disabled students are placed in their classroom.

15. The Whites have been instrumental in organizing a group of parents of special education students. At a meeting last week, thirty-one people had turned out to hear a local advocate speak on inclusion. A number of these parents have severely disabled children assigned to self-contained special education classes. Two of them have children who are multiply disabled and who are presently attending special private schools. If the group were to continue meeting, they could become a potent force within the school district. The Whites had been a driving force behind the first two meetings, but up until now, no official organization had been established.

The superintendent considered the ways that the school district could react to the problem presented by Charlie White's placement. It seemed these were the following options:

a. He could suggest that Linda recommend the placement in a fourth-grade class. If Mrs. Hensen would not agree to accept the boy, another fourth-grade teacher should be given the assignment. Should all of the teachers seek to avoid the assignment, there was one nontenured young teacher who would undoubtedly accept the challenge.

b. The district could refuse the placement and accept what other consequences might follow.

c. The district could suggest a trial placement that would be reviewed by the committee after the first quarter of the school year.

There might be other options and Bill had at least until tomorrow to think about them.

## POSSIBLE DISCUSSION QUESTIONS

1. Is there additional information that should be gathered before the committee meets?

2. Should the superintendent be concerned about the possibility of alienating some faculty members with an inclusion placement of this sort?

3. Should the superintendent be affected in his judgment by the formation of the parent's group?

4. Can you think of any additional ways to deal with this decision?

5. What should the superintendent say to the psychologist when they meet?

# Case Study 17

# Merit Pay

Compensation plans for administrators, teachers, and staff members are often a topic of discussion within school districts. The issue can be raised in Board of Education meetings or when a district is at the negotiating table, and there are often major disagreements over how salaries should be determined. Board members who work in the private sector frequently feel that all employees should be paid based on how well they do their jobs. These individuals believe that, with modifications, the models used in business can be emulated by school districts. Many teachers and their professional organizations have been wary of plans that attempt to define and reward excellence in teaching and as a result, many employee groups have preferred to not even explore the subject. In this case, a newly elected Board of Education member is insisting that a merit pay plan be implemented.

Only last night Tim O'Malley had said to his wife how well things had been going in the district. During the past two years of his seven-year tenure as superintendent, the school district had been moving forward. Test scores were up, morale was high and the community seemed quite happy with their schools. As an experienced superintendent, Tim was aware that this state of affairs could change quickly. The district had seen stormy periods in the past when the Board of Education and their employees had been at odds. Within the next several months, negotiations for new contracts would open with the Administrators Organization, a group of twelve administrators excluding Tim and his assistant superintendent. A month after these talks were scheduled to begin, negotiations would open with the four hundred-member teachers' union.

Tim had not been overly worried about the upcoming contract talks until the recent campaign for a seat on the Board of Education. The winner, Blaine Clark, was the executive vice president of Taylor Industries, the largest and most influential business in the district. The new board member had lived in the community for three years and had gained the reputation of being a tough, dynamic leader with many new

ideas. Although he was somewhat controversial, there was no question he was helping the business to prosper. While he had earned the respect of some residents, others saw him as a "hard and unfeeling hatchet man." Whatever his image, he had been
able to defeat his two opponents in the election by a comfortable margin. During the
campaign, he had spoken forcefully about bringing good business practices to the
school district. Although he had not been openly critical of Tim and his administration, Blaine had emphasized that many of the practices that had been used to make
Taylor successful could also help the school district.

During his campaign appearances, Blaine had often spoke of instituting a merit
pay program for the employees of the district saying, "If we can tie compensation
to performance, we cannot help but to improve the quality of the school." He
hinted that there were district employees who did not deserve an automatic
annual raise, and remarked at one board meeting that employees should not be
given an increase "just because they became a year older."

Several of the teachers had heard these comments and Blaine was quoted in
faculty rooms around the district. The union president, Jim Lewin, said to Tim the
day after one of Blaine's speeches, "Does this mean that we have to talk about
merit pay again?" Both Jim and Tim remembered that during Tim's first contract
negotiations with the teachers, the board had presented a merit salary plan. After
weeks of fruitless debate, the district had dropped the idea, but the withdrawal of
the proposal had not come until after the union had picketed a board meeting.

The administrative unit was no more enthusiastic than the teachers about a
merit plan. Since all of the administrators had been teachers, they, too, were comfortable with the salary schedule that guaranteed raises for at least the first fifteen
years on the job. Tim, whose salary was determined after his annual evaluation,
could not quite understand why the administrators were unwilling to even consider alternatives to a salary schedule. The Board of Education had treated him
fairly and he expected that they would be equitable with their other administrators as well. Each time the issue came up, several of the senior administrators told
the story of how they had been compelled to form their unit a decade ago. At that
time, a majority of the Board of Education had apparently been somewhat
unsympathetic to the district's administrators. For several consecutive years,
administrators' raises were less than those of other employees, so the administrators had formed their own bargaining unit and were now represented by a paid
staff member of the statewide president's organization. Three years ago, Tim had
taken it upon himself to negotiate with this representative of the principals and
because at that time the climate in the district was quite positive, a contract had
been accepted by both the unit and the Board of Education in just four meetings.
The superintendent was well aware that the new board member would want the
administrators to be paid based upon their performance.

Blaine had called Tim two days after his election to ask him to put the issue of
"merit pay" on the agenda for his first official meeting. Although Tim had tried to
persuade Blaine to wait until the board formally began preparing for negotiations,

the new member insisted that the discussion begin right away. He reminded Tim that this had been an important plank in his election platform and that he was committed to "moving on the issue." When the superintendent told him about the history of merit pay in the district, Blaine merely said, "We will find a way." Tim had suggested that, because it was a potential contractual issue, the board should discuss it in an executive session. Again, Blaine disagreed and forcefully explained that he wanted the voters to know that "he was going to keep his promises."

Tim could recite the upcoming arguments in his sleep. The employee groups would argue that "schools are not businesses. . . . You cannot adequately quantify the job being done by teachers and principals. . . . Who is qualified to make the judgment on teaching effectiveness? . . . Should a principal who does not speak Spanish judge a Spanish teacher? . . . It is not fair to rely on tests. . . . Even a qualified administrator who comes into the classroom only three times a year cannot fairly judge a teacher's contribution to the school district. . . . Are you going to rely on parents who are not even in our classrooms? . . . Is it fair to use the evaluations of students who care primarily about their grades? . . . Teaching is an art and there is no one right way to teach. . . . If some teachers get a merit bonus based on unfair evaluations, it will undermine morale and foster competition rather than cooperation in the classroom. . . . It just cannot be done fairly."

Blaine and other board members would say that most of the evaluation problems raised by the employee groups were not unique to schools. It would be his position that if the district and unions worked together, they could develop a mutually acceptable plan. Perhaps there could even be a component which included "peer evaluations," but the teachers would undoubtedly respond that they had neither the time nor the expertise to judge their peers and that such a system would only sow distrust within the faculty and the administration. The board member would probably ask, "Why do we have administrators if they do not evaluate the people who work for them?"

This might not be the exact dialogue, but these arguments would undoubtedly be put forward. As the debate continued, it was possible that tempers would flare and the level of tension between the Board of Education and its employees would grow. If Blaine was able to convince a majority of the board to pursue the issue of merit pay in the upcoming contract negotiations, Tim saw nothing but stalemate and trouble. Maybe something could be worked out with the administrative unit, but he did not see the teachers changing their position. Tim's immediate problem was to plan for the public discussion that would take place at the next Board of Education meeting.

## POSSIBLE DISCUSSION QUESTIONS

1. What should be Tim's long-term strategy for dealing with the issue of merit pay in the district?

2. It appears that Blaine Clark is going to be a forceful and perhaps difficult person. How should the superintendent attempt to deal with the newest board member?

3. What should the superintendent say publicly about this issue at the next board meeting?

4. Should Tim plan to be the chief spokesperson in the negotiations with the administrative unit?

5. What role do you think a superintendent should play in formal contract negotiations with an employee bargaining unit?

## Case Study 18

# They Just Can't Keep Their Mouths Shut

Whenever a group of people share confidential information, there is a good chance that the secrets will eventually become public knowledge. In school districts, there are times when secrecy is called for. Administrators and board members are frequently privy to personal information concerning faculty and staff, or have knowledge of such issues as the district's position in contract negotiations. While statements made in executive sessions are not usually meant for the public or the press, participants in these meetings are occasionally guilty of sharing information with others. When this happens, people become overly cautious and untrusting, which can adversely affect the decision making process. Dealing with the problems of Board of Education confidentiality can be a very sensitive issue for a superintendent.

It seemed to Superintendent Marie Dolman that there were at least three members of the Board of Education who were unable to keep confidential discussions that took place during executive sessions to themselves. Then again, the problem could lie with one of the administrators. The fact was Marie really had no idea who was talking publicly after meetings. She was quite sure that it wasn't Board President Kent Levy. Kent had been as upset as she with the "leaks." Both of them had, on several occasions, cautioned those present at an executive session that a certain fact must remain confidential. Months would go by without a problem and then another incident would occur. The most recent transgression was the worst yet.

A local reporter had run a newspaper story attributed to a source present at a recent executive session of the Board of Education. The story suggested that a member of the custodial staff at the middle school was being investigated for starting a series of fires in the school that had disrupted classes and had been widely reported in the newspaper. The local police were furious about the story, because now everyone knew that a custodian was being considered as a suspect, and all four building custodians had come to Marie to complain.

This was not the first personnel discussion that had become public knowledge. A review of two probationary teachers who were having some difficulty with discipline was a topic of discussion in the faculty room two days after the Board meeting. Within a week, the rumor was going around that these teachers would be released at the end of the year. When someone casually mentioned in a private meeting the possibility of putting out a bid for the cafeteria program, the rumor circulated that the district would be firing its cafeteria staff and would contract with McDonalds. These types of stories undermined morale within the district.

During a discussion about the percentage wage increase the district would offer to bus drivers, the board had decided the offer should be 3 percent. A quick settlement with this group of employees was desirable, so they had authorized their negotiating team to offer 3½ percent, but only if "absolutely necessary." It did prove to be "absolutely necessary" and several weeks after the contract was signed, Marie learned that the bus drivers' negotiation team had known about the 3½-percent figure when they entered the meeting.

There were a number of other times when confidential information had become public knowledge, but Marie had always avoided checking into them. When she considered some kind of private inquiry, she always backed away from investigating her own colleagues. It was clear to her that the reporter who covered the district would not reveal his sources and she did not feel comfortable quizzing faculty, staff, and parents about how they had gained their information. At this point, she knew that something should be done.

## POSSIBLE DISCUSSION QUESTIONS

1. If you were faced with a similar situation as an administrator, what course of action would you take?

2. Confidentiality is only one area of concern when people become board members. If you were devising a list of topics which might be included in an orientation for new school board members, what other topics would you include?

# Raising Test Scores

In almost every state there is increased pressure for school accountability. The most recent yardsticks by which a school's effectiveness is measured are the results on standardized tests. Scores on these examinations are increasingly featured by the media and because of this growing public scrutiny, school administrators are seeking ways to raise test scores. Administrators can help to provide the resources, but in the end, the responsibility for raising test scores lies with the students and teachers. A school, department, or grade level whose examinations do not meet the expectations of the community can create serious problems for an administrator.

Ron Lucas had never found his position as department chair at Lincoln Junior-Senior High School difficult. He felt close to all of the other six science teachers in the district; the group worked well together and often socialized outside of school. Their families were well acquainted and at least a couple of times a year, the group would come together for a picnic or a dinner. As a department, they had a reputation of being not only harmonious, but also effective. Each teacher specialized in one area or grade level, and Ron's twenty-six years as an eighth-grade teacher made him the senior member of the group. During his long tenure, he had participated in selecting each of the other teachers and everyone in the department felt that, as a group, they provided the school with a superior science program.

The peace and good cheer that had pervaded the department might now be disturbed. As he poured himself a cup of coffee in the small department office, Ron recollected the meeting he had just left with the other department heads and the principal. The purpose of that gathering had been to review the recently released results of the new statewide achievement test. The examinations were given in every high school subject and comparative scores were about to be made public. For many years, Lincoln Junior-Senior High School had enjoyed a reputation as the best academic high school in the county. With an average family income above $75,000 a year, residents paid high property taxes and they expected a quality program in return. Compared to most other high schools in the area, Lincoln had excellent academic standards. At least 85 percent of their graduates went on to college each year and many of them attended the best colleges in the country. At the meeting, Principal Beth Miller had stressed the high expectations of the parents of the district and focused only on what she and the superintendent considered the "trouble areas." One of those areas was in Ron's science department.

After pointing out the problem, Beth, in front of his fellow department heads, had said that Ron should "light a fire under Oliver Roberts." It seemed that the average score of Oliver's eleventh-grade chemistry students had only been 80.4 percent. The average in the county schools on that test was 83.7 percent. It was the only score in the science department that was below the county average and only three other scores in the entire high school had dropped below the average scores of neighboring schools. Two other department chairs had also been told to do what was necessary to ensure that next year, these scores were above average.

Ron had always thought of Oliver Roberts as the most creative and committed teacher in the department, if not the entire school. As Ron thought about it, there were several possible explanations why Oliver's students' scores were lower than at other schools. Chemistry was not a required course for students who did not intend to go to college, but Oliver's class was so popular that even non-college-bound students chose to enroll. In other schools, such marginal students often decided not to take chemistry. In addition, Oliver had a higher percentage of students in the junior class taking the exam and that could adversely affect the average score of his students.

It was also true that he refused to "teach for the test." When the new statewide tests were introduced, most teachers modified their curriculum so that only those topics contained in the state syllabus were taught; science teachers chose only to do the minimum number of labs allowed by the state. Most teachers had finished their curriculum four to six weeks before the test and had used the final weeks for the review of practicing old test questions.

In the chemistry classes at Lincoln Junior-Senior High School, nothing had changed since the new examinations were introduced. Oliver continued to enrich his course by taking class field trips to a local chemical plant and a science museum in a nearby city. He still gave frequent writing assignments and had students do research on famous scientists and share their reports with the rest of the class. Since the test was primarily objective in nature, the writing assignments did not particularly help his students prepare for the chemistry examination. Still, Oliver believed students should have the opportunity to write and to speak in front of a group. He graded every paper carefully, always emphasizing the fact that a student's English skills were extremely important.

Oliver also loved to have class discussions. Ron had visited classes in which the students were discussing whether science was a "body of knowledge" or a "method for finding truth"; another time, the students were talking about a "scientific theory" as compared to a "law of science." Both the students and Oliver found these inquiries fascinating and also enjoyed their teacher's stories about the lives of famous chemists.

There were also several labs that, while not required, Oliver refused to give up because they were a great deal of fun for the students. As a result of his teaching style, a large number of the chemistry students at Lincoln learned to love chemistry, and many of them entered the county's annual science fair, where they often won prizes. Time was also taken in class for students to share their projects. These activities and the teacher's personal magnetism had been instrumental in leading dozens of his students to major in chemistry in college. Five of his former students now held Ph.D.s in chemistry and three had gone on to become physicians.

With this creative approach to his course, Oliver had little time in the spring to review for the statewide test and in fact, had let it be known that he didn't like the test format. He saw it primarily as a test of a student's memory, rather than an assessment of a student's ability to problem solve. As a result of his own excitement about the subject and the positive feedback he had received through the years from his students and their parents, Oliver had never worried about the state chemistry test.

Ron knew that approaching this topic with his friend would be extremely difficult. Although Oliver was usually very mild mannered, he was extremely sensitive to any kind of criticism. Ron also knew that the chemistry teacher was likely to talk to all of his friends about the issue and that the problem might well upset others in the department. Most of his colleagues would be sympathetic, but at least two would probably support the administration. Oliver was a bit too independent for these two colleagues and perhaps even slightly arrogant. Ron wanted to deal with the issue in a way that would not endanger the good feelings that were always present in the department. He also wanted to ensure that his personal friendship with Oliver was not harmed. He needed a plan.

## POSSIBLE DISCUSSION QUESTIONS

1. Should the department chair go back to the principal and attempt to explain the reasons for the lower average test scores in chemistry?

2. Should this problem be seen as a departmental issue or dealt with privately between the department head and the teacher?

3. If you were Ron Lucas, how would you deal with this issue?

# Case Study 20

# The Bomb Scare

Periodically, schools are plagued by false alarms or bomb scares. It is necessary, of course, to have in place a written procedure for dealing with these kinds of disruptions, and administrators must be extremely careful in dealing with such incidents. Most often, the problem is caused by a student who is seeking for some reason to disrupt the school. In this case study, a school administrator is faced with a decision as to what to do about a call that he believes does not constitute a real threat.

Anthony Latini had been an assistant principal for seven years and he had spent many nights at the school, and tonight he was there for the third consecutive evening. His boss, Principal Don Bowler, was out of town, leaving Anthony on duty for all three performances of the student production of *Oklahoma!* On Thursday and Friday evenings, the cast had received a standing ovation and this final performance had seemed to Anthony to be the best yet. With the last act just beginning, the assistant principal decided that he would take a brief break in his office. He knew that there were four faculty chaperones in and around the auditorium and that everything was going well. As Anthony entered the office, the phone had been ringing. Thinking of the week that had just passed, he almost let the call go unanswered. After five rings, it occurred to him that it could be an important call for someone in the auditorium. As he picked up the receiver, it had flashed through his mind that the call might be from the same young person who had called earlier in the week. On both of those calls, the voice had been described as that of a young person between the ages of nine and twelve. Now Anthony heard the voice say, "This time it really is a bomb," and when he tried to engage the caller in a conversation, the individual hung up.

As an administrator, Anthony knew that he was supposed to call the local sheriff and evacuate the building. It was the middle of January, the wind chill factor was below zero, and he was loath to have the fifteen hundred people in the auditorium wait outside until the sheriff arrived. Earlier in the week, the school had been emptied twice in order to search the building. The first time, the students were sent home early. When the second call came through, it had been pre-arranged to bus the students to the elementary school and the firehall. Following the hour and a half search, they were brought back to the high school.

It was now 9:45 P.M. and the play would be over in thirty to forty minutes. If Anthony cleared the building, he knew that it would be after 11:00 P.M. before the sheriff's deputies would allow people to reenter. He also questioned the thoroughness of the search process, because although the sheriff's department had a dog that was supposed to be able to find a bomb, it would be almost impossible for Anthony and two sheriff's deputies to do an effective search.

Angry and frustrated, he didn't really believe that this child had planted a bomb in the building. By evacuating the school, he would be disrupting the final performance that the students had worked months to prepare. There were several hundred senior citizens in the audience and it wasn't practical that they should be expected to stand outside in the cold. It could be suggested that they wait in their cars for an hour and a half, but this seemed unreasonable. Those in the audience had spent $6.00 for the ticket to the performance and Anthony wondered if he should offer a refund. Perhaps people could be allowed to come back on Sunday to see the final act, but district policy prohibited school activities on Sundays without the permission of the Board of Education. Would people even want to come back to see the last thirty minutes of the show?

If only he had not come down to the office, no one would have been there to answer the phone. What if this young person was right and there was indeed an explosive device in the building? Was that even possible?

## POSSIBLE DISCUSSION QUESTIONS

1. What are the possible alternatives of the assistant principal?

2. What should he do?

## Case Study 21

# Sexual Harassment

In recent years, especially since the confirmation hearings of Clarence Thomas, the issue of sexual harassment has been a prominent topic in every type of organization, including schools. Incidents involving teachers and students, administrators and teachers, and between students have been highlighted in the local and national media. Most school districts have now established mandatory staff development programs as well as policies that assist victims seeking redress, and school administrators play important roles in their implementation. In this case study, the sexual harassment victim is a teacher and the accused are students.

Mary Davis was the assistant superintendent of schools for personnel, but she had a number of additional responsibilities in the Forest Hill School District. One of her newest assignments was to act as the sexual harassment policy officer for the district. In this capacity, she was to be the first person who would receive reports of alleged sexual harassment from students, faculty, or staff. Her role was to first listen to the person's complaint, which at this stage would remain confidential, and then informally seek to resolve the issue. Mary had received special training to prepare her to work toward solutions that would avoid formal charges and possible litigation. Thus far, she had successfully handled several complaints using the mediation techniques she had learned. A respected administrator in the district, Mary had the employees' trust and with five successful years in the middle school classroom, she had learned to work well with adolescent students. Yet despite her success to date, Mary knew that the case before her now was different.

Leonard Bennett was in his fifth year as a middle school math teacher and at age twenty-eight, he was a studious, intense young man. Through careful organization and planning, he had overcome the discipline problems of his first year of teaching and had become a successful teacher. His math students scored well on standardized tests and his fellow teachers had learned to respect his commitment to the profession. Although he spoke softly, the students in his classroom were generally well behaved. It was widely known that he could become angry and that students who became the object of his wrath should beware.

The young teacher had visited Mary's office late in the day of the previous Friday. Most of the faculty and staff had left for the weekend and Mary was herself about ready to pack her briefcase and leave for home. Shyly, Leonard asked if Mary could spare him a few minutes. She could tell by his demeanor that he was both nervous and upset. He told Mary that he was there because of her position as the sexual harassment policy officer in the district. The problem was that a group of boys were tormenting him in the halls of the school. On three separate occasions when he was walking to class, a group of three or four seventh and eighth grade boys would make comments under their breath such as "there goes the queer". . . "I wonder if he is going to meet his boyfriend" . . . "everybody look at Forest Hill's resident queer!"

It had been difficult for Leonard to know for certain which boy was making the comments, but he was convinced that the leader of the group was Kyle Sinclair. An eighth grader, Kyle was almost six feet tall and a star on the middle school basketball team. Although he was not a great student, he did have a following among the students and was known as the toughest kid in school. On the other hand, Kyle was also very involved in the Boy Scouts and had been instrumental in doing several projects that were beneficial to the community. His father was a Boy Scout leader who was well known and respected in the community. Leonard was convinced that if someone could affect Kyle's behavior, the harassment would stop. The last incident had brought the teacher close to chasing the boy down the hall and grabbing him. Leonard was sure that other students had heard what the boys said and felt that, unless it was stopped immediately, the problem would only get worse. The young teacher was close to tears on that Friday as he told Sally that these boys were "going to ruin his career." He had said, "Teaching is my life and if I am run out of here by these kids, there will be nothing left."

On Monday morning, Mary confronted Kyle and investigated the boys who might be involved and was not surprised when they all claimed innocence. Kyle did say that "everyone knew that Mr. Bennett was a queer," but that he had never called him one. Mary had given the boys a lecture about the sensitivity of the issue and how it was absolutely wrong to refer to someone in this way. She told them about the law regarding sexual harassment and the possible penalties that could follow. Mention was made that parents might have to be involved. Her goal had been to try to ensure that the boys understood fully the implications of their alleged behavior. They said nothing when they left her office, but Mary was very uneasy about the conversation. She was not sure what to do next.

## POSSIBLE DISCUSSION QUESTIONS

1. Should Mary go back to Leonard and try to identify witnesses to the incidents in the hall?

2. Should she notify the boys' parents of the allegations?

3. If you were Mary, what, if anything, would you do next?

*Case Study 22*

# Promotion from Within

Some education professionals climb the administrative ladder by moving from district to district, while others are promoted from within a system. Each route to advancement creates its own challenges. For a person promoted from within a district, the historical baggage of events and relationships can affect one's ability to lead. Starting with a clean slate is impossible when an administrator brings to the job old friendships and rivalries, and how a newly appointed administrator begins can be crucial in determining success or failure.

Kevin Gates was not altogether surprised when Superintendent Jean Benson asked him to consider accepting the position of high school principal. Within the past few years, the school had had two short-term principals who had been hired from outside the district. Sheila Radcliffe had been a disaster. The first woman principal in the school's history, she had felt that it was necessary to be tougher than any man. When the district's very effective woman superintendent pointedly suggested that she might be more sensitive and compassionate with people, Sheila could not accept the advice. Within two years, she had managed to alienate large numbers of faculty, students, and parents, and almost everyone was happy when she resigned and left the district.

The second outsider had been Jim Ripkin, a young man with the potential to be an excellent administrator. It soon became evident to many staff members that his outside interests were more important to him than the job, and after two years, he resigned to pursue his own private business.

With the history of these two failures, it was not surprising that the superintendent and the board began to look within the district for their new principal. Only three secondary faculty members had completed the course work and internships necessary to qualify them for the position. Of these individuals, Jeffrey Bowman was the respected chair of the English department. An excellent teacher who also showed great aptitude for management, Jeffrey had acted as interim principal on several occasions and demonstrated considerable ability in the role. Although he was an obvious choice, Jeffrey was not interested in the job. Had it been offered five years ago, he probably would have accepted, but now, at sixty-two years of age, he and his wife were actively making their retirement plans.

The second potential qualified candidate was Ann O'Riley. As the district athletic director, Ann, too, had shown considerable aptitude for management. She was well organized and enthusiastic about the school's interscholastic athletic program. As the coach of the girls' basketball team, she had been successful in producing winning teams for years, and for this reason, she was well known in the community. Unlike Jeffrey, Ann was interested in the job. Unfortunately, her potential candidacy was strongly opposed by a significant number of faculty members. It was their opinion that her role as physical education teacher, athletic director, and coach had resulted in Ann's lack of knowledge about and insensitivity to the academic program. However unfair this perception might have been, numerous teachers had privately informed the superintendent that Ann was an unacceptable choice.

This had left only Kevin Gates, the chair of the history department, as a viable candidate. He had taken the necessary courses to be certified as a school administrator two years ago and at that time, he had been very anxious for the opportunity to be a principal. As the years passed, he had all but given up the idea and now, at age forty-five, with twenty years experience in the district, he was being given the opportunity to lead the school. During his twenty years in the district, Kevin had made many friends on the faculty. He and his wife, Marge, had entertained many of the teachers in their home, and it was not unusual for the families to go on weekend outings together.

Kevin served three two-year terms as president of the local teachers' union and on several occasions had represented the teachers at the bargaining table. As a vocal champion of teacher involvement in decision making, Kevin could not help but wonder how he was going to make the transition to being part of the management team. Undoubtedly, his friends were also thinking about this question.

It was also true that not everyone on the faculty was his close friend. As a union leader, Kevin had unquestionably been a moderate, and when a grievance arose, he had always tried to solve the problem informally, without resorting to lawyers and formal hearings. He had also preferred to use tactics other than picketing and public confrontation in order to reach contract settlements, as he believed that such strategies were often counterproductive. This aversion to confrontational tactics gave some teachers the impression that Kevin was a weak leader, afraid to take on the power structure. Perhaps his most important leadership rival was Dennis Kelly, who, like Kevin, had also served several terms as president of the union. There had seemed to be a higher level of conflict within the district during Dennis's administrations, with open clashes between Dennis's supporters and those, like Kevin, who were uncomfortable with more combative strategies.

As he was about to begin his new position as high school principal, Kevin had many friends, but also a minority of teachers who did not admire him. Likewise, in the community and on the Board of Education, there were individuals who did not support his appointment. During the next week, Kevin would have the opportunity to address both the faculty and the Parent Teacher Association. He knew that first impressions were important and he wanted to begin well. He also was feeling more nervous about these upcoming meetings than at any other time since his first year of teaching.

## POSSIBLE DISCUSSION QUESTIONS

1. What actions should the new principal involve himself in during the week before school opens?

2. Should he attempt to have private discussions with selected faculty or community members in the district?

3. Note the themes that you believe Kevin might highlight in his initial speech to the Parent Teacher Association.

4. What themes should he include in his speech to the faculty on opening day?

## Case Study 23

# The Six-Pack

The consumption of alcoholic beverages in schools and at school events is a problem that is faced by almost every high school in the United States. Most secondary
schools have a written policy which includes the procedures which are to be followed when a student is accused of breaking the rules in regard to alcohol. For a
student to consume alcohol at a school event, in most cases, would be considered a
major infraction. Although policies certainly would differ, it is not unusual that one
infraction involving alcohol could lead to suspension. Sometimes, it is difficult to
prove that a student has actually consumed alcohol and in the case that follows,
more is involved than just a short term suspension. High School Principal Jane
Price had always felt that the senior picnic on the Friday before Sunday's graduation ceremony might someday be a problem and this was to be the year. After the
picnic, the senior class advisor, Bill Johnson, had brought four boys into Jane's
office. The dilemma he described was unlike anything she had faced in her five
years as principal.

After spending eight hours at a nearby amusement park and beach, Bill had been
ready to return to school the three busloads of tired seniors. The students had had
a picnic at noon and then been allowed to move about the park for the rest of the
day. Before giving the signal to begin the hour-long ride, Bill had instructed the
chaperones on each bus to take attendance. Four boys were missing from the lead
bus. Someone had seen the foursome heading into the picnic area an hour earlier,
so Bill decided to search that section for the boys. He saw them sitting around a
picnic table and he quickly but quietly walked toward the group. They did not
observe his approach and when he was close enough to hear their voices, he saw
Lance Betters look at his watch and say, "I don't know, guys, but I think we are
supposed to be back on the bus. Let's drink up!" Lance was taking a drink out of
a can of beer as Bill joined the group at the picnic table. In front of the boys on
the table was a six-pack and four empty cans of beer. Along with the one that
Lance had been drinking, there was another half-full can on the table.

Bill dumped out the remaining two cans on the table and put all of the empty cans in the carton and told the boys to accompany him back to the bus. Nearly all of the seniors saw the teacher carrying the cans as they returned. Bill assigned the boys to seats in front of him, where they remained silent on the ride home.

Not only did the four boys remain quiet, but the entire busload of seniors, obviously aware of the problem, was subdued during the entire trip. A few minutes before they arrived, Lance blurted out, "Mr. Johnson, what's going to happen?" Bill merely replied that they would be visiting Mrs. Price when they got back to school.

When the class advisor and the boys entered the high school office, Bill asked the students to remain in the outer office while he talked to Mrs. Price. Explaining to the principal what had happened, Bill noted that he had only seen Lance drink the beer. When asked whether he had smelled any beer on the breath of the others, Bill apologized for not thinking of doing that at the time. He also admitted to the principal that he had not questioned the other three boys about whether they had consumed any of the beer. When he had come upon them at the table, the surprised chaperone had assumed that the boys had been sharing the six-pack. After listening to Bill, Jane decided to question the boys separately, beginning with Lance. She first asked him whether he had drunk any of the beer from the six-pack that was now sitting on the principal's desk. His response was that he knew Mr. Johnson had seen him take a sip, and that was all he would admit. When Bill, who was still in the office, asked Lance where the beer had come from, Lance answered that he had brought the six-pack in his knapsack. Jane then queried the boy on whether the other boys had consumed any of the beer. He quickly responded by saying, "You don't really expect me to rat on them, Mrs. Price? They are my friends!" Bill was now getting upset and he interjected, "Lance, you don't expect us to believe that those three guys sat around and watched you drink almost the whole six-pack?" Lance put his head down and merely said, "You can believe what you want." Watching him closely, the principal did not feel that the boy showed any signs of intoxication.

Her interviews with the other three boys were all the same. Jane asked to smell their breath and all of them had obviously been sucking on breath mints, so she could certainly not swear that she smelled beer on their breath. When each of them was asked where the beer had come from, they all said that Lance had brought it from home. Each of them denied having even taken a swallow of the beer. Exasperated, Jane began to bear down on the final boy interviewed, Ben Gordon. When he sensed that she was going to press him, Ben had asked to call his father, who was a successful attorney in the village. Jane reluctantly decided to end the questioning.

Following their interviews with the boys, the advisor and the principal reviewed the situation. Bill noted that all of the boys were from affluent families, and although they were not among the top academic students in their class, they had all been accepted at private colleges. Jane expected that their families had planned large graduation parties over the weekend, and relatives would be undoubtedly be coming for Sunday's graduation ceremony. Having recently read through the awards to be given during the program, Jane recalled that at least two of the boys were scheduled to be publicly recognized.

Before releasing the boys, she had instructed them to tell their parents about the incident. She said she would expect both the boys and their parents to be in her office tomorrow morning at 9:00 A.M. With graduation on Sunday, a decision would have to be made after that meeting. One of the boys, Pete Dawson, had asked as he left the office whether it was all right to bring an attorney to the meeting in the morning. Jane knew that if a long-term suspension were to occur, the students would have such a right and she informed Pete that this was appropriate. The principal told the boys that she would give them two hours to inform their parents before she called them to officially invite them to tomorrow's meeting. Before Bill left, he apologized to Jane for the way he had handled the situation. She responded by pointing out that she had made the biggest mistake by allowing the boys private time together to prepare a story. While she had been listening to Bill's report, it was quite possible that the boys had agreed that Lance would take the blame and that the others would deny doing any drinking. Jane attempted to reassure the teacher that he had done a good job.

As she considered her predicament, Jane realized that she needed to read over the policy regarding the student use of alcohol. Having dealt with the problem a number of times, she easily found the page in the student handbook. The policy stated that, "When a student is suspected of bringing alcoholic beverages to school or to an off-campus, school-sponsored activity, or of consuming alcoholic beverages in school or during a school-sponsored activity, the student will be scheduled for a formal hearing before the superintendent of schools or his or her designee. If found guilty of violating this policy, the student will be placed on suspension for a period of not less than five days." While reading the rule, it occurred to Jane that a suspension in this case would mean none of the students could participate in the graduation ceremony, as a suspended student was barred from school-sponsored events.

Given the facts, it appeared that at least Lance would be suspended and prohibited from being part of the graduation ceremony. Jane's boss, Superintendent Tom Oliver, was not going to appreciate having his graduation weekend spoiled by this incident. Both he and Jane had been invited to a number of graduation parties and they also would be busy in last minute preparation for the ceremony itself.

Tom Oliver was a stickler for details when he conducted a disciplinary hearing. He always wanted the principal to have a solid case and this was especially true when the students' parents brought a lawyer to the hearing. Of course, the superintendent did have the prerogative to employ an administrator from another district or perhaps a retired superintendent to conduct the hearing. Jane thought she might suggest this to Tom, but she was not sure how he would react to being advised to try to avoid the issue. It was also possible that the school attorney should be brought in on this case. Although he was on a retainer, there would be an extra charge, yet Jane felt she would be more comfortable if the district had its lawyer at the hearing. Even though it might interrupt his supper, she decided to call the superintendent, but before she did so, it occurred to her that she should be prepared to suggest a course of action.

## POSSIBLE DISCUSSION QUESTIONS

1. What, if anything, should the school authorities have done differently up to now in this situation?

2. Assuming that a formal hearing does take place, should Jane insist that the school attorney be brought into the case?

3. Should the district enter into any agreement that would allow the students to participate in graduation?

4. What do you feel should be the strategy of the school administration in this case?

*Case Study 24*

# A Career Decision

Administrators aspiring to more responsible and higher-paying positions are often faced with difficult choices as they seek their career goals. A frequent decision that confronts an administrator is whether to remain in a district and wait for an opening to occur or to move to another school district where there is an immediate opportunity. Often, there are uncertainties surrounding each of the options. Family concerns and a spouse's career can be factors in the decision and if the administrator is a parent, the wishes of children should also be considered. For the ambitious administrator, every career change should be evaluated carefully. You must ask yourself whether or not the job being offered will help you move closer to your career objective.

To his acquaintances, Phil Carson was known as a "young man with a future in educational administration." For the past four years, he had been the very successful principal of Littlefield Elementary School. With an enrollment of five hundred and sixty students, Phil had made it one of the most respected schools in the area. The teachers and students enjoyed his enthusiastic and intelligent leadership style and the current Board of Education members already considered him the probable successor to Superintendent Linda Kincaid. The superintendent, who was now fifty years old, had often said that on her fifty-fifth birthday, she and her husband would be off on a round-the-world trip, so there was little question that she planned to retire as soon as she was eligible.

In Phil's mind, his future was quite clear. He wanted to become a superintendent and he was confident that by the time Linda retired, he would be ready to assume her position. He felt confident that even if Linda were to leave today, six of the seven current board members would support his candidacy for the superintendency and he would be even more qualified when he completed his Ed.D. at the local university. It had occurred to him that during the five years before Linda's retirement, there would undoubtedly be several new board members and possibly additional rivals for the job. During that period, both the middle school and the high school principals would retire. Although neither was interested in becoming a superintendent, their replacements might well be, but even with this potential competition, Phil felt confident about his future in the district.

This contentment did not keep him from being flattered when a friend from a nearby district asked him to consider being a candidate for the vacant middle school principal job in suburban Glenville. This school included grades five through eight and had 1,115 students. Along with the added challenge of a larger school came an annual salary that was $16,000 higher than he was currently being paid and $1,000 more than his current superintendent's salary.

The school building in Glenville was extremely attractive and the faculty was the highest paid in the area, but it would be necessary for Phil and his family to eventually move. Besides the fact that Glenville "strongly urged" their administrators to live in the district, the hour-and-a-half drive to and from his new school was out of the question. He and his family would have to move from their small, comfortable farmhouse in the rural community to a more affluent, suburban area.

Despite the many questions in his mind, he decided to apply for the position and at least go through the interview process. He told his wife, Kathy, what he was doing, but pointed out that he was only one of nine candidates being interviewed for the job. When he was chosen as one of the three finalists, Phil knew it was time to sit down with Kathy and their two daughters to discuss the possibility of moving to another community, but they were very busy and the family discussion never occurred. When, after the interview, the Glenville superintendent called and offered him the job, Phil was somewhat caught off balance. He did think to ask for a few days before he gave a final answer.

The young administrator was excited, but also a little nervous when he told Kathy about the offer. Together they began to think of the factors that would affect the final decision. Kathy immediately thought about her own job as an accountant. If the family moved to Glenville, her commute would include about fourteen miles of additional driving each day, including about five miles of driving on a somewhat congested superhighway. The total commuting time would increase from twenty minutes to thirty five minutes each way.

Their two daughters were asked about their feelings regarding the move. Melanie was a well-adjusted sixth grader who was somewhat apprehensive about leaving her friends. Phil and Kathy knew that she would fit in easily wherever she went and if she were given a veto, Melanie would not have voted against the move. Jennifer was a first grader who was much less outgoing than her sister. Although a quiet child, she was currently doing well and was already reading at a fourth-grade level. She was not enthusiastic about the prospect of moving, but Jennifer certainly would not create a fuss. She appeared quite relieved when she learned that both her dog and cat could come along. Kathy summarized the family discussion by saying that, although everyone was quite happy living and going to school in Littlefield, the women in the family could accept Phil's decision to take the job in Glenville. After the family meeting, he decided to go to his study to think about his career decision.

There was no question in his mind that he could be content to live the rest of his life in Littlefield. He would very much like to be the superintendent of schools sometime in the near future. Admittedly, he would be very upset if he waited five years until the position was vacant and someone else was chosen for the job. He knew that Board members changed often and it was possible that four of the seven could in five years favor someone else. This was especially true if two outstanding, experienced principals were brought into the district during the next three years. It was too far in the future for him to be overly confident that the superintendent's job would someday be his. The Glenville position, although not a superintendency, paid better than the position he was aspiring to in his own district, though whether this would still be true in five years, he did not know. On the other hand, a move to another principalship could be considered à lateral move. Of course, Glenville Middle School was a much more prestigious principalship than his current position. He wondered how the position in Glenville would affect his ambition to be a superintendent. Perhaps he could work five years in Glenville and go back to Littlefield as superintendent when Linda retired. It was also possible that by then, he would have been forgotten in his old school district and that one of the three newer principals would be a more likely candidate. Having left the district, he might be considered an opportunist who had "burned his bridges." The board might also think that he had left once and would be likely to do so again.

As he considered his options, Phil knew that the challenge of the new school appealed to him. He was confident that he was ready to be principal of a larger school. Of course, he had put a lot of time and money into his doctoral program and would need a considerable amount of time during the next five years to complete his dissertation, which would be easier to do if he stayed in Littlefield. Although he knew his family was likely to adjust to a new community, it was evident to him that they were all happy in their current home. Secretly, Phil also worried that if he stayed, he might grow restless as Littlefield's elementary principal during the next five years. He had already become accustomed to the annual events and was afraid that he might find himself saying the same things at the science fair, PTA, and faculty meetings. He also knew that the budget would continue to be tight and that innovation would be hampered by a lack of funds. In Glenville, he would have not only ample financial resources, but expert help with curriculum and personnel. Another advantage of the new job would be that he would have two assistant principals to help him keep up with his workload. This could mean perhaps less evenings out and considerably less time spent with minor student disciplinary problems. Clearly, this was not going to be an easy decision.

## POSSIBLE DISCUSSION QUESTIONS

1. What are the primary factors one should consider when making a decision on a new job?

2. Which of Phil's alternatives might most likely lead to his goal of becoming a superintendent?

3. What would you decide if you were in his position?

*Case Study 25*

# Do We Really Want to Have a Union?

State laws vary in regard to the right of administrators to form unions and to engage in collective bargaining. Traditionally, administrators have been considered to be part of the management team of the district. Decisions on salaries and fringe benefits for principals and other administrators were usually made by the Board of Education. Often, the superintendent would act as the primary advocate of all the administrators in the district. Before teachers began to negotiate for their own salaries, administrative compensation was most often much greater than that of faculty members. With increased militancy and collective bargaining by teacher groups, the financial settlements with faculty in many schools have outstripped the raises given to administrators. As a result, it is now not unusual for veteran teachers to make as much or more money for a ten-month schedule than a principal is paid for working twelve months. This trend has caused administrators across the country to become more assertive in seeking to improve their conditions of employment. Even some smaller school district administrators have taken advantage of collective bargaining laws and they have formed their own unions. Yet for some principals, the idea of administrative unions has been distasteful and someone with these feelings might well ask a colleague, "Do we really want to have a union?"

It was John Lewis who was attempting to persuade his colleagues to petition the Board of Education to recognize the five principals in the East Dryden school district as an official bargaining agent. Under state law, any group of school employees that was not considered "confidential" could seek such recognition. Once granted such status, the group gained the legislative right to formally negotiate the "terms and conditions of employment." This negotiation would create a formal contract listing salaries and fringe benefits, as well as such other issues as vacation days and leaves. The final result would be a legal contract that would be signed by both parties.

John explained to his colleagues that their unit would be entitled to utilize the services of a professional negotiator from their state Principals' Organization. If this occurred, the board would most likely hire their own professional to represent them. He also pointed out that the contract would include a grievance procedure that would help the principals resolve differences with the district. He and High School Principal Tony Lombardi were convinced that the current board was actually somewhat antagonistic to their principals. Although the five principals were all making between $55,000 and $65,000 a year, their salary increases during the past three years had been no more than the rate of inflation. Unlike the teachers in the district, the principals were not paid for extra duties, such as chaperoning a dance, even though they were often back at school for evening events two or three nights a week.

All of the administrators in the district were feeling that their hard work was too often "taken for granted" by the Board of Education. At the same time, the teachers' union was pushing the board for increasingly higher salaries and other financial "extras." While teachers were now being paid more if they completed graduate courses, principals were given no such remuneration. There was no question that during the past three years, the financial compensation of teachers had dramatically outstripped that of the administrators. During this period, teachers' salaries had increased 15 percent, while the principals had seen only a 9 percent growth. The principals were also extremely sensitive to the fact that they were expected to work 225 days per year, as compared to the teachers' 185. John Lewis had calculated that a large percentage of the faculty was being compensated more per day than their supervisors.

At a recent administrative meeting, the five principals had brought these facts to the attention of Superintendent Bob Kindred. Although sympathetic, Bob was not the type of superintendent who would enjoy clashing with the Board of Education over such a volatile issue as administrative salaries. To the principals, his past requests on their behalf for additional compensation for administrators lacked the assertiveness needed to gain the approval of board members. For most of the board, administrators' salaries were higher than their own family income, so they had little sympathy for people who thought that a $60,000-a-year salary was inadequate.

Elementary Principal Kate Lincoln was not really worried about her salary all that much. After five years in the district, she and her husband had a combined income of well over $100,000 per year. For her, working in the district was a great joy, she and her school had received significant recognition in the community, and the work atmosphere was positive. She enjoyed an informal and cordial relationship with both the superintendent and the Board of Education. Kate recoiled at the idea of being part of a union. Her father had been a shift supervisor at a local automobile assembly factory, and as a child, she had heard stories of arrogant shop stewards, frivolous grievances, work slowdowns, and even strikes. Kate knew that Tony Lombardi had very different feelings about unions. His father had been a union officer at the same plant and had told Tony stories of how high paid managers had taken large salary increases at the same time they were laying off workers. While Kate had been a well-dressed, upper class student in high school, Tony had been from a working class neighborhood. She had gone to a well-known private college and he had worked his way through community college and a state teachers' college program. Tony and his wife had five children and his wife was a full-time homemaker. Living on one income, the family was trying to save enough to send their children to college in a few years. Despite their different backgrounds, Tony and Kate were good friends and she understood his support of the proposal to form a principals' union.

On Friday afternoon, the five principals were planning to meet to decide on a course of action. There was no question about the opinions of John and Tony. The feelings of Middle School Principal Kelly Davis and elementary principal, Dan Richards, were unknown to Kate as both of these individuals were relatively quiet at meetings. Kate, on the other hand, was prepared to challenge her colleagues who were seeking to organize a bargaining unit and during the meeting would ask, "Do we really want to have a union?" As the meeting approached, she could not help but wonder what she would do if she ended up in the minority on this issue. Would she refuse to join and jeopardize her relationship with her peers? Would she be forced to be part of the union if three of the other principals supported it? Whenever she thought of a union, all she could picture in her mind were picket lines, nasty negotiations, and possibly a strike. How could she associate herself with such a group? Would membership adversely affect her excellent rapport with the Board of Education, the superintendent, parents, and other faculty? Was there a better way for principals to achieve their objectives? Kate was not looking forward to the meeting.

## POSSIBLE DISCUSSION QUESTIONS

1. What should be Kate's strategy at the meeting with her fellow principals?

2. Do you believe it is professionally appropriate for school administrators to organize unions?

3. When such unions are formed, what tactics are acceptable by the group in attempting to achieve its objectives?

# He Didn't Do Anything Wrong!

If we are to believe survey responses of secondary students, cheating is widespread in our schools. Besides copying each other's homework, students frequently find ways to not only plagiarize, but also to buy term papers. Every school administrator will deal with students cheating during his or her career and if the school has an unambiguous policy, it will be easier for the disciplinarian. Unfortunately, it is difficult and perhaps impossible to devise rules to govern every possible situation. As a result, like a judge, the administrator must seek fair and just solutions to difficult problems.

Bob Lake and Jim Childs had been close friends for most of their fourteen years. Growing up in the same neighborhood, they had attended elementary and middle school together. They had played on the same Little League team and now, as high school sophomores, were teammates on the junior varsity baseball team. Although the boys were the best of friends, they were different in many ways. Bob was an honor student who, as a sophomore, had been inducted several months ago into the Senior Honor Society. He was extremely interested in his academic subjects and both he and his parents had high hopes that he would someday attend an Ivy League college. Like most young people, he had changed his mind several times, but currently he was hoping to become a lawyer. His excellent writing and speaking skills undoubtedly would help him to succeed as an attorney.

Jim Childs, on the other hand, was a C student in every subject except industrial arts. As a junior next year, he planned to enter a vocational program in carpentry. He would spend half a day at his high school to take his required academic courses and then be bused to the vocational school for the afternoon. Since he had not really enjoyed most of his classes in middle school and high school, Jim was looking forward to the carpentry classes where he was sure he could earn excellent grades. Before he could attend the vocational class next year, he had to pass all of his tenth-grade subjects. He was doing fine in math and science, but English and social studies were difficult for him. Secretly, he was fairly certain that his tenth-grade social studies teacher, Mr. Smith, would give him a passing grade. He and Mr. Smith got along very well and often talked outside of class. They had a mutual interest in supporting the New York Yankees and for Jim, Mr. Smith was "a cool guy." He couldn't help but think that if he continued to do his homework regularly, he would pass social studies.

His English teacher, Mrs. Olson, was another matter. Jim often had difficulty understanding his English teacher's discussions of literature being considered by the class. Although he liked her, she was just "too smart." When the class would read a poem or a story, she would find so much to talk about in class and brought up ideas that had never occurred to him when he read the material. He did read the assignments and even enjoyed some of the books, especially after they were explained in class. Although he remembered reading *Tom Sawyer* and feeling that he understood the author's point, he felt almost totally lost during the poetry unit. While Jim enjoyed Edgar Allen Poe and Robert Frost, he was totally confused when he tried to read Chaucer or Milton. It greatly concerned him that he couldn't attend the carpentry class until he passed tenth-grade English. Jim was not at all confident that Mrs. Olson would give him a passing grade. In English class, he had said very little and he knew she had not been impressed with his written work. His papers always came back marked up, with comments that seemed to indicate that he was missing some of the main points in the story or poem. He was able to pass her daily quizzes on the reading assignments, as the questions were always factual. It was difficult for Jim to interpret literature and throughout the year, exam essays and other written assignments had been problematic. For the first time in his school career, he was worried about actually failing a course.

As the year came to a close, Mrs. Olson had been out of school with bronchitis during the first two weeks in June and the substitute teacher had continued the unit on John Steinbeck's book, *Of Mice and Men.* Upon Mrs. Olson's return, a number of students voiced their opinion that the substitute had been incompetent. Mrs. Olson knew her substitute had probably been less than inspiring, but the students, for their part, had not been overly cooperative. In any case, there was not adequate time left during the school year to both reteach the book and review for the final exam. After considering her problem, Mrs. Olson decided on a novel compromise. During the last week of school, she decided to give the students a take-home test to be turned in on the day scheduled for the English exam. When she distributed the test, which consisted of all essay questions, she instructed that students were not to work together and that the work must be their own.

When Jim read the test questions, he saw that there was a twenty-five point essay on the book *Of Mice and Men.* He had not really understood the book and the substitute teacher's class discussion had not helped. When Mrs. Olson returned from her illness, she had taken one period to review the entire novel, and although Jim had taken notes, when he sat down to write the test question he couldn't even understand them.

Two days before the test was to be turned in, Jim and Bob were walking home from baseball practice. Jim asked Bob how he was coming on "Olson's test" and Bob replied that he had finished the essays the night before. On the rest of the walk home the boys talked about their last baseball game, which was to be played the next day.

That night, sitting at his desk with a copy of *Of Mice and Men* and a blank sheet of paper, Jim decided to call Bob. When Bob picked up the phone, Jim said, "Talk to me about *Of Mice and Men.* You always understand this stuff and it's always Greek to me." Bob responded by saying, "Sorry, buddy, I'm on my way out to a movie with Jill, but I'll tell you what I'll do. I'll drop by and let you look at my essay, just to get a couple of ideas. Maybe it will help you to get your mind in gear." Jim had not even thought about actually looking at Bob's essay, but when Bob stopped by, Jim took the essay back to his desk.

Over the weekend, Nancy Olson had read the two essays at least three times. There was no question that whole sections were almost identical in each essay and she was sure that the ideas were Bob's. The boys were very close friends and Bob was a superb English student, while Jim had struggled throughout the year just to earn a passing grade. Even though he was a very quiet student, Nancy liked Jim and knew that he really tried, even with his poor writing skills, he had obviously read the material and passed her daily quizzes. Up to this point, she had fully expected that he would earn a C in her class. Still, it was obvious to her that the essay on *Of Mice and Men* on the take-home test was not his work. It was equally clear that Bob had somehow been involved with the preparation of Jim's test. Unsure of what to do, Nancy decided to show the two essays to her principal, Carol Lanigan. After reading the two papers, the principal agreed that cheating had occurred and immediately summoned the boys to her. It was a very short conversation. Carol confronted the boys with the two papers and stated that it was clear that someone had cheated. "Who is going to tell me about it?" she asked. After a short period of silence, Jim admitted that he had looked at Bob's paper and had copied some of it for the test. When the principal asked how Jim got the paper, Bob was quick to say that he had given it to his friend. As the discussion continued, Jim admitted that he had panicked when he couldn't come up with any ideas for the essay. He knew what he had done was a mistake and he was also quick to point out that his friend Bob "didn't do anything wrong."

With the boys on their way back to class, Nancy and Carol began to consider an appropriate course of action. The student handbook was not much help. There was a paragraph about the seriousness of cheating and plagiarism, but the consequences for such acts were not clearly delineated. Carol admitted that most often, these incidents had been handled by classroom teachers on an individual basis. In this case, Nancy was asking the principal's help in resolving the issue.

## POSSIBLE DISCUSSION QUESTIONS

1. Should schools attempt to develop definitive policies on cheating and plagiarism? If so, what forms should such policies take?

2. If you were recommending a punishment for Jim, what would be your decision?

3. Should Bob be punished for his part in the incident?

4. How would you attempt to make this a learning experience for both boys?

*Case Study 27*

# What Happened
# to Academic Freedom?

Reading materials assigned by classroom teachers can be a source of conflict within a community. Frequently, the issue relates to what parents feel is inappropriate language or overly graphic sexual passages. At other times, the source of controversy can relate to a religious topic. There is often a high level of emotional involvement by the participants and the school administration and Board of Education are often placed in the position of mediators or arbitrators in such disputes. Many teachers are protective of their right to choose the materials to be used in their classrooms and are sensitive to any effort to interfere with what they consider academic freedom. At the same time, parents feel that they should have the veto power on what their children read in school.

Wendy Linderman wanted to read a new and more contemporary play this year with her eleventh grade students. During her first five years as an English teacher, she had chosen for her twentieth century play, Arthur Miller's *Death of a Salesman*. Although the play provided a vehicle for discussing the shallowness of people's lives in the twentieth century, Wendy had the feeling that her students last year had not really been excited about the play. Even though the class had been assigned parts and had acted out some of the scenes, several students confided to her that they thought the play was slow and depressing.

After reading a story in the newspaper about a conflict in a southern school district, Wendy had the idea for a new play. The news story had been written about a religious organization that was demanding that the creationist view be included in the school science curriculum. Beyond the school district in question, there was growing support from evangelical Christians throughout the state to mandate that the Christian view on creation be taught in all biology classes. These individuals were not seeking to replace the teaching of Darwin's theory of evolution, but asking that the Biblical interpretation of creation also be taught. Although the state science teachers' organization opposed the addition to the curriculum, there had been Christian teachers throughout the state speaking out publicly in support of the idea.

With this controversy in the headlines, Wendy thought it would be a perfect time to have her students read the play *Inherit the Wind*. The plot of the play revolved around the famous Scopes trial held in Tennessee in 1925. That year, the Tennessee legislature had passed a law making it illegal to teach "any theory that denies the story of the divine creation of man as taught in the Bible." John T. Scopes, a biology teacher in Dayton, Tennessee, agreed to challenge the law, with the support of the American Civil Liberties Union, by lecturing to his class on Darwinism. Clarence Darrow, the famous brilliant, but cynical, defense attorney and a religious skeptic, offered to defend Scopes. William Jennings Bryan, the former Democratic nominee for President and defender of the fundamentalist Christian viewpoint, agreed to lead the prosecution.

Although there was no question that Scopes had violated the law, this did not define the importance of the trial or the drama of the play. During the defense of Scopes, Darrow put Bryan on the stand and pilloried him mercilessly on religious issues. This famous cross-examination of Bryan was featured in the play and to many Christians who had read the play or had seen it on the stage, it seemed to be mocking their faith. Wendy had seen the play as a teenager and recalled the dramatic moment in the final act where Bryan's character collapsed in what was to be his stage death. For her, it was great theater, entertaining, yet socially relevant and she was sure her students would love it. She planned to set up the classroom like a courtroom, and thought about just the right students to play the major parts. Maybe they could even perform a scene from the play for an assembly program.

All of these plans were now set aside. Two days after she distributed the play books to the students, a delegation of five parents had visited the office of the principal, Roberta Standish. After that meeting, Wendy had been told to collect the books and, for the time being, not to discuss the play any further. The parents, who were all members of the local Baptist church, had brought the play book, with large sections of dialogue highlighted, to the principal's office. There was no question in their minds that the play was anti-Christian. They noted that while the character based on William Jennings Bryan was portrayed as a fool, the playwright had pictured Clarence Darrow as humorous and wise. The scene in which Darrow cross-examined Bryan was clearly making fun of the Holy Scripture, and the law-abiding citizens were made to look like narrow-minded bigots. The parents were certain that reading the play would undermine what the young people had been taught in Sunday School. They went on to say that there were many others who were upset with the play and that if the teacher did not desist, there would be a "huge" turnout at the next Board of Education meeting, including several of Mrs. Linderman's students opposed to the play.

After the parents' visit had forced Wendy to change her plans, a number of her students had come to their teacher's defense. Lance Farley told a local reporter that the play was "awesome." He said that he didn't think it was at all sacrilegious and couldn't figure out what all the fuss was about. Other students commented publicly that Mrs. Linderman was a great teacher and that she was just trying to make the class "interesting and relevant."

It wasn't long before others in the community entered the fray. An attorney was quoted in the newspaper asking, "What happened to academic freedom?" and one parent told a reporter that she "did not want a bunch of religious fanatics deciding what her children could read in school." Ministers and priests, whose positions were varied, felt compelled to comment from their pulpits on the controversy. A local bookstore had sold one hundred copies of the play in twenty-four hours. Within the school, there were several heated debates, both in the student cafeteria and the faculty dining room. The president of the teachers' union had written a letter to the Board of Education defending academic freedom and the "right" of Mrs. Linderman to use the play in her class. The controversy was being heavily covered by the media, and reporters and television cameras were expected at the upcoming board meeting.

At least three of the board members, because of their church affiliation, might be sympathetic with the protesting parents. Prior to that meeting, Mrs. Standish and her superintendent, Ron Blakeman, would have to be prepared to take a position on the controversy. For both of them, this was the biggest crisis in their careers as administrators.

## POSSIBLE DISCUSSION QUESTIONS

1. What steps should the administrators take in preparing for the public Board of Education meeting?

2. How could this crisis have been avoided?

3. Once a decision is made on this situation, what should the school district do to ensure that this problem does not occur again in the future?

Case Study 28

# To Join or Not to Join

Many Boards of Education expect that school administrators will be active participants in community activities. As they are often among the most visible and highly compensated public officials, administrators are sought out by various groups as potential members. Membership in community organizations offers administrators, in their roles as spokespersons for the school district, an important way to communicate and build support for their schools as well as cultivate the personal support of influential community members.

Even with these advantages, community involvement can place unrealistic demands on an administrator's personal life, especially if the activities require frequent meetings. Coupled with an administrator's many evening commitments at school, the additional civic responsibilities can create a schedule which has the administrator away from home four or five nights each week. Finding a proper balance is an important challenge faced by most school administrators.

Jim Price was a first year superintendent in the Washingtonville School District. At age thirty-four, he was one of the youngest superintendents in the state. He was also one of the few with three children still in elementary school. His son, John, was twelve years old, Hannah was ten, and the youngest, Mike, had just begun first grade. Margaret, his wife, was a third grade teacher in a neighboring school district. The Price family had been in Washingtonville for only four months when Len Scott approached Jim during a refreshment break at the Board of Education meeting. Len was the vice president of the board and had been one of the new superintendent's chief supporters when the board was selecting their new officer. A sales manager in the district's largest company, he was very active in community affairs and the most assertive member of the group.

At the board meeting, Len had asked Jim to consider joining the local Kiwanis Club. One of the three local service clubs, the Kiwanis was the most active and prestigious organization in the town. The members were involved in numerous service projects, including such aid to the school district as a lucrative scholarship and funds for field trips, computers, and library materials.

Jim had already learned that his predecessor, Bill Gray, had been an active member of the club for almost twenty years. While other members of the school administration had participated in the past, none of the current principals had been willing to join and so the school district was unrepresented. It was obvious to the superintendent that the Kiwanis Club was an important group and that its continued support would be very helpful to the school district. Politically, Jim knew that he was expected to join and become an active member, but when Len offered the invitation, Jim had hesitated and asked for a week or so to discuss it with his wife.

Although their discussion that night did not lead to a decision, it was clear that Margaret had some major reservations about his potential membership in the organization. As a new superintendent, Jim was already averaging three evening events per week. On these nights, he usually saw the children for just a few minutes, and on days when there were dinner meetings, he sometimes did not see them at all. It was already clear that his three children would be active in community athletics and scouting, and Jim would have only a limited number of evenings free to participate in these activities. As a former athlete, he really wanted to have time to coach a baseball or soccer team, but even with his present schedule, this seemed unlikely. Looking ahead, he could see that community involvement could even keep him away from his children's school events. He wanted to be there when they were inducted into the Honor Society or playing in a basketball game.

In her kind way, Margaret also brought to his attention that she was already doing most of the childrearing and housework. Most evenings, she didn't get to plan her lessons or correct papers until after 10:00. She was especially concerned when she learned that the Kiwanis met every Tuesday evening, all year long, and if you missed a meeting, you either made it up by attending another meeting in a neighboring community or paying a $10 fine. In addition, there were committee meetings and weekend work projects to attend. Despite the fact that the Prices were a double income family, they had not yet saved very much for the children's college education or for supplementing their retirements. There was no question that membership in the club would be an added drain on the family budget. Following their brief midnight discussion, Jim thought that it was safe to say that Margaret was not enthusiastic about him being out another evening each week.

Jim had his own reservations about membership in the organization. During his first month on the job, he had been invited to speak at one of their meetings. The members had all been friendly and the speech had gone well, but he had not been entirely at ease. He noticed that, both before and after the meeting, a large number of the members spent time at the bar. This was a practice he knew he would not be comfortable participating in on a regular basis, and wondered if he would be expected to take part in this ritual.

The format of the meeting also had surprised him. Both before and during dinner, which itself cost $12, the presiding officer maintained an ongoing banter with the membership that resulted in some rather heavy fines. Although it was done in fun, it was evident that the fines were providing a great deal of revenue for the club treasury. It really was not the potential cost of membership that most bothered Jim, but rather the overall atmosphere of the meeting. He would not enjoy the kidding and joking, nor the fraternal courtesies required when addressing fellow members. He was basically a quiet man whose primary interests were artistic and intellectual, and he would feel better serving on the library board or on the board of directors of the Arts Council, even though these organizations did not have the political importance of the Kiwanis Club. The fact remained, however, that a portion of his evaluation form alluded to community involvement. There was no question the board saw such activity as an important aspect of his job.

Even with these additional pressures, Jim was not ready to accept an invitation to be a member of the club. This was an important decision for him and his family that could have an impact on his career. Tomorrow evening, he would be seeing Len at a meeting and he needed to be prepared with an answer.

## POSSIBLE DISCUSSION QUESTIONS

1. Is it appropriate for a Board of Education to expect the superintendent to be involved in the community outside of school events?

2. Is it politically advantageous for an administrator to be active in community affairs?

3. How can a principal or a superintendent balance such activities with school obligations and family life?

4. What would you do if you were in Jim's situation?

5. If you choose not to be part of the organization, what would you say to the board member?

*Case Study 29*

# Choosing an Architect

School administrators often take the lead in selecting other professionals to serve their districts. Whether choosing a school attorney, accountant, or architect, the district must devise a fair and efficient way for deciding on such appointments. When choosing a person or firm to serve the district, there is often pressure to hire locally. Dealing with local individuals and companies can help the school district's economy and gain additional support for the school program, and, as taxpayers, local people may have additional motivation to do a good job.

On the other hand, dealing with local people can create problems if the project or job does not go well. It is also true that smaller local firms often cannot offer the same level of services as a larger outside company. Whether or not it is good policy, however, there will always be pressure to hire from within the community.

The sketch of the proposed new middle school submitted by the Acker and Sons architectural firm looked familiar to middle school Principal Susan Stankovich. It looked like the new village fire hall the firm had designed two years previously, which was the only major project the architects had ever worked on. Most of their work during the twenty-one year history of the firm had been remodeling and building a number of one-story cement block office buildings. The school project would have six times as much square footage as the fire hall, but the design was little more than a plain, rectangular building which looked like a factory. The sketches of the interior of the building also showed little or no imagination.

As a former art teacher, Susan could not understand how the superintendent and the Board of Education could possibly be thinking of hiring Acker and Sons to draw the detailed plans for the new middle school. She had taught both of the sons in her junior high art class and neither had shown any aptitude for design as students. She didn't know their father, but judging from the sketches, she was not impressed. In comparison, the proposals submitted by two larger firms from a nearby city were both creative and exciting. They envisioned buildings that middle school children would enjoy entering. Their floor plans included a variety of room sizes, each of which would help make the school a better place to teach and learn. Both of the larger firms had also included necessary storage spaces. As the principal of the new middle school, Susan would be proud to give tours of the new facility, and she knew that her pride would be shared by students, faculty, and parents, as well.

Susan knew her superintendent, Ray Miller, and the Board of Education must be under pressure to select Acker and Sons. She remembered the board's discussion in executive session when the district was hiring an accounting firm. In that case, they had requested bids for accounting services and the local accountant's bid was higher than a firm's from the city. It was heard through the grapevine that the city accounting firm sent its "inexperienced, twenty-one year old auditors" to do outside work, which proved to be reason enough to throw out the low bidder and accept the local account. During that discussion, several board members who were businessmen in the community spoke with great emotion about the need to support local enterprises. Susan remembered one member saying, "The school is the biggest business in our community and we spend millions of dollars each year. We need to keep as much of this money in the school district as possible. The businesses will do right by us. Remember, it is their school and they don't want to cheat it."

There was an opposite point of view expressed at the meeting. One older member of the Board pointed out that, "Our school taxes are already too high. Senior citizens are having to sell their farms and homes because they can't afford the property tax. We have to run this school district like any business. This includes shopping around to get the best job at the best price. We cannot afford to give charity to local professionals and businessmen." Thinking back, Susan remembered the emotions engendered over the decision on hiring the accountant. She could envision a similar problem occurring with the selection of an architect. However, there was one major difference in the two situations. In the case of the accountant, the problem was not a question of competence but that his bid was higher than the competitor. With the middle school project, the architectural services bid of Acker and Sons was the lowest of the three bids, but competence rather than price was the concern. There were other issues that also had to be considered. Both of the larger firms had engineering departments. If Acker received the bid, the school district would either have to hire an engineering firm itself or entrust its architect to select the engineers for the project. Having the same firm providing architectural and engineering services would avoid potential conflict between the two. In addition, the two companies from the city had presented a long list of references of former clients, as well as pictures of schools they had previously designed. Both had received awards from trade journals for several of their past projects.

Susan knew that, as a woman, she would not be expected to know anything about mechanical drawings and architecture. Actually, she had a keen interest in both and felt certain that she knew more about building a school than her boss and probably any of the members of the Board of Education. As an administrator who lived outside of the community, she also knew she might be at a disadvantage when arguing about whether or not the school district should favor the local firm. Looking again at the Acker design sketches, she was infuriated that this company would even be considered, but she knew there would be an intense debate and probably a close vote on the selection of an architect.

Given the fact that she was a nontenured administrator, Susan didn't know whether she would hurt her career if she was too outspoken at the upcoming meeting. She felt that the superintendent would not hold it against her and would merely want to reach a consensus and have everyone leave the meeting happy. On the other hand, those board members who were affiliated with the Chamber of Commerce and personal friends of the Acker family could be upset by any criticism. Theoretically, none of this was Susan's problem since as principal, she was to administer the new building, not design or build it. She could always "play it safe" and just keep quiet. Although this might be possible for some school administrators, Susan knew she would have difficulty keeping her opinion to herself.

## POSSIBLE DISCUSSION QUESTIONS

1. Should school districts give any special consideration to local professionals or companies? If so, what guidelines should the school district follow in making these decisions?

2. How should Susan make her opinions known on the architectural decision?

3. If she decides to speak at the Board of Education meeting, what should she say?

# Case Study 30

# A Tough Act to Follow

Whether one's predecessor in a position was popular or unpopular, a new administrator is always the object of comparison. While it can be advantageous to follow someone who was disliked, succeeding a venerable and loved administrator presents "a tough act to follow." In such a situation, the new administrator must plan carefully his or her initial weeks on the job. This case study deals with a young superintendent in this difficult situation.

Emmett Adams, a legend in his community, had retired after serving forty-two years in the Clarkson Central School District. A teacher and a principal in the district, he had been appointed superintendent thirty years ago. At that time, there were 750 students in grades K through 12, and Dr. Adams had seen that number grow to nearly 5,000. During his long career as a superintendent, seven bond issue campaigns had been successfully conducted and four new school buildings had been constructed. It was rumored that the board would rename one of those buildings The Emmett Adams Elementary School.

With the exception of three veteran teachers, Dr. Adams had been involved in the hiring of all 250 faculty members. Nearly every teacher respected and revered the man who had helped to make Clarkson an outstanding school district. As an individual with a phenomenal memory, he knew all of the faculty and staff members by name and often knew something about their families. As the chief school officer, he frequently complimented district employees on their accomplishments and his graceful personal notes were treasured by those who received them. Dr. Adams took notice of new family members and always paid his respects when an employee had a death in the immediate family.

Four of the current members of the Board of Education remembered Dr. Adams when they had been students in the high school and all of the board members were deferential to the superintendent. Although it was common knowledge that he had been slowing down in recent years, there had been little public criticism,

100

even when he had begun to fail. He had talked more about the past than the future and some younger, more liberal faculty members had believed him to be too conservative and resistant to change. While his administrative team had tried to pull him into the computer age, he had refused to have a computer in his own office and continued to hire secretaries who took shorthand. His aversion to technology had led Clarkson to fall behind other area schools in introducing computers as instructional tools, as well as a means for improving the efficiency of school offices.

Dr. Adams had also been very slow to raise salaries. He was proud of never having a budget request defeated and kept salaries down to ensure continued community support. As a result, both the teaching and nonteaching staff had salary schedules that were among the lowest in the state. In addition, to keep property taxes low, class sizes had been increasing in recent years and while this practice had generally been accepted in the school district, there were a number of people who understood the imprudence of this trend.

It would be the challenge of the new superintendent, Aaron Poole, to deal with these and other difficult issues. Coming from outside the district, he soon learned that Dr. Adams would be "a tough act to follow." At age thirty-five, he had already shown that he could be an effective leader and was chosen after a long search from over one hundred candidates. Aaron had been the superintendent in Cedarville, a small district with 1,100 students, and came to the Clarkson position with a reputation as a creative and innovative administrator. An active speaker in the region, he was known as one of the up-and-coming administrators in the state.

His interviews in Clarkson had been positive and it seemed to him that it would be the right administrative move at this stage in his career. He had enjoyed Dr. Adams and had spent several afternoons listening to his stories about the history of the school district. Almost everyone he spoke with on his visits to the community had been positive about the future of the district. He had now been in his office for just three days and had made a list of the problems he would have to address.

1. There was no unified policy manual. To find board policy on any issue, it was necessary to search for a copy of the board minutes for the meeting in which the policy had been adopted.
2. Salaries needed to be improved. The employee groups would soon begin to push the superintendent and the Board to make their compensation more competitive.
3. The average age of the faculty was almost fifty and most of the teachers had been in the district for their entire careers. Many were in the "count down" to retirement and were not really interested in participating in major change.
4. There had been very little money spent on staff development for faculty members.

5. The district property tax owners were accustomed to the lowest tax rate in the county and were generally satisfied with their schools. Additional spending would seem to many to be unnecessary.
6. There was one computer for every 200 students. None of the district administrative offices were effectively using computers.
7. The enrollment of the district was continuing to grow and the average class size had reached twenty-six.
8. The school libraries had not been kept current. In browsing the middle school library, Aaron had found a history book that claimed in its final chapter, "Undoubtedly, some day, the United States will have a man walking on the moon."

Aaron was sure that the list would grow even longer. Next week, he would be addressing the faculty at the opening meeting and would have his first meeting with the Board of Education. What should he say about the challenges facing the district? Would his comments be interpreted as criticism of his predecessor? How long would he be able to avoid discussing these problems? As the new superintendent, he felt it would be a mistake if he attempted to make changes too quickly. Knowing himself, Aaron was sure that he would have difficulty merely being a caretaker administrator. There was much to accomplish and he was eager to get on with the task.

## POSSIBLE DISCUSSION QUESTIONS

1. Could Aaron have found out more about the district before he agreed to take the job?

2. What is generally the best strategy for a new administrator during the first few months in a new district?

3. What, if anything, should the new superintendent say in his initial meetings about the problems facing the district?

*Case Study 31*

# We Will Not Have Our Child
# in That Woman's Class!

Determining which elementary students will be assigned to a teacher is a problem that all schools face. There are a number of ways this decision can be made and each method has its advantages and disadvantages. One procedure is to assign the students in a totally random manner. Although it appears to be fair, this approach can lead to an unbalanced classroom where, for example, a particular teacher could receive a large percentage of discipline problems. A second technique is to allow the students' current teachers to meet and make what they feel are appropriate assignments. In this way, the student's personality can be matched with the teacher who can best deal with the child. In some elementary schools, the principal and the guidance counselor are actively involved in the process. Whatever method is used, it may lead to parental protest. A key question faced by most elementary schools is how much, if at all, a parent's preference should be considered in assigning a child to a particular classroom. This issue can be especially explosive if at a certain grade level there are extremely popular or unpopular teachers.

Lou Gillespie had thought that in his new job as an elementary school principal, the summer would be a relaxed time. The teachers and students were gone and all he needed to do was to prepare for the coming year. However, his hopes for a stress-free summer seemed to be wishful thinking. He shuffled through the seven letters on his desk and read them for a second time. All of the letters were from parents of next year's fourth graders, and although they differed greatly in their level of sophistication, each was making the same request, or in some cases, demand. They were unanimous in the desire to have their children transfer from Miss Melroy's fourth-grade class to another teacher. Five of the letters specifically asked that their children be placed in Miss Montgomery's class.

The assignments for next year's fourth-grade classes had been made at a meeting of the third-grade teachers. Knowing the strengths and weaknesses of their colleagues in the fourth grade, they attempted to match the student to the most appropriate teacher. This procedure was followed at every grade level and most years had been successful. Of course, there had always been some unhappy parents. Gwen Smith, the previous principal, had always worked individually with parents who had requested a change and had occasionally made a switch in the original assignment. These infrequent transactions had been done without involving any of the faculty or any of the four superintendents Miss Smith had worked with over the years.

In the current situation, the fourth grade teachers were also concerned about the placement decisions. There were difficult children at every grade level and no teacher wanted to be saddled with them. In recent years, the academic abilities of the students assigned to a class had also become an issue. Since year-end testing results were now public knowledge, every teacher wanted to have as many academically able students as possible. Faculty members often complained that they had been assigned an extraordinary number of students with learning disabilities.

Lou Gillespie had been a sixth-grade teacher before he was appointed principal, and had just finished a successful first year as the school leader. The problems he had faced had all been quite manageable and he believed he was well on his way to earning the respect of the faculty and parents. He knew that with this current dilemma, he was likely to make someone unhappy. Reading the letters made it clear to him that Miss Melroy had obviously lost the confidence of a number of the school's families.

During her thirty-two years as a fourth grade teacher, she had earned the reputation of a "no nonsense" faculty member. During his five years as a colleague, Lou had noticed that Miss Melroy had become increasingly critical of the children in her class. She spoke of their lack of ability to concentrate and their frequent disrespect for authority, and in faculty meetings she complained about the "modern parents" who didn't try to control their children. Her teaching style remained very traditional with an emphasis on phonetics, and drill and practice in her math classes. Her language arts classes were based totally on the Basal Reader and its workbook. Despite frequent workshops, she had not been convinced that any of the concepts embodied in whole language instruction should have a place in her classroom and she did not accept the value of student projects, interest centers, or cooperative learning. While the other fourth-grade students talked to their parents about science projects and videos they had seen, Miss Melroy's students reported that they had done "the same old thing." Her former principal, Miss Smith, had made suggestions through the years, but in the end, she let Miss Melroy do things her way. The slightly higher than average test scores in reading and math had convinced the principal not to interfere.

Until recently, Miss Melroy's methods had been accepted by most parents and some conservative families had even sought to have their children assigned to her. This had also been true for some families whose students had been discipline problems in the third grade, thinking that she might "whip their child into shape."

This had begun to change three years ago when the parents of one of her students had complained that Miss Melroy had "physically abused" their son. When Tommy Adams had refused to take his seat when he was told to, Miss Melroy had apparently then taken him by the arm and forcefully placed him in his chair. Mr. and Mrs. Adams not only complained to Miss Smith, but they also wrote a letter to the Board of Education, and a number of rumors were spread about Miss Melroy's discipline methods. She submitted an apology as requested by the board, and although the issue was ended by a mild letter of reprimand placed in her personnel file, the incident damaged Miss Melroy's reputation in the district.

This past February, another problem was alleged to have occurred in her classroom. John Curtis, a serious discipline problem within the school, had accused Miss Melroy of slapping him. According to John, he had been "fooling around" and Miss Melroy had ordered him into the hall. While she was yelling at him, he told her to "bug off" and "she slapped me in the face." Miss Melroy had vehemently denied slapping the boy, but admitted to grabbing him by the shoulders to gain his attention. Unlike the previous incident, Mrs. Curtis had not complained. She told Lou that whatever happened, John had probably deserved it and she admitted to the principal that she could not always control her son at home. In addition, she told Lou that John sometimes made up stories. Given the fact that there were no witnesses, Lou had in the end merely cautioned the teacher about even touching the students. He had put another mild letter in her personnel file, but decided that there was nothing else that he should do. Word of the incident spread very quickly, and there was no question in the principal's mind that those rumors had something to do with the seven letters on his desk. He had made some notes of direct quotations when he had reported the problem to Superintendent Bill Hanson, and it seemed a good idea to review these sentiments before he considered a course of action.

- Miss Melroy is a perfect example of why we should do away with teacher tenure. She should not be allowed to work with our children.
- Obviously, this teacher no longer has the self control to be in the classroom.
- Our Lindsay is a very sensitive child and would not be comfortable with a drill sergeant for a teacher.
- We have already had one child who had to endure a year with Miss Melroy. She did not like our son Robert and we don't want our daughter to also have a bad year in the fourth grade. We want her put in Miss Montgomery's class. One family should not be punished twice.
- It's not fair that some children have a positive, creative and caring teacher, and others must experience one who is negative, boring and potentially violent.
- Many parents don't care who their children have as a teacher. We do care and we don't want our son in Miss Melroy's class.
- We will not have our child in that woman's class!

These quotations represented just a few of the more outspoken excerpts from the letters. The problem was complicated by the fact that, although there were four fourth-grade teachers, five of the letter-writers had specifically asked to have their children assigned to Miss Montgomery. She was a young, third-year teacher who had quickly developed a positive reputation in the district. Her student projects often included parental participation and everyone who met her was impressed with her enthusiasm for teaching and her obvious love of the students in her class. One fourth grader had summed up the students' view when she told her parents, "Miss Montgomery is cool!"

No one had ever accused Miss Melroy of "being cool" and if they had, she would not have seen it as a compliment. Lou knew that the veteran teacher had devoted her life to teaching and he didn't want to hurt her. He was also aware that she was on tenure in the district and that, with the exception of the two alleged corporal punishment incidents, there was little that was negative in her personnel file. In fact, for most of her career, the reports on her classroom observations were quite positive. There certainly was not a record which would support the dismissal of a tenured teacher. He had reviewed the file with the superintendent and they had both agreed that there was no basis for charges alleging incompetence. When their discussion had ended, the superintendent had asked Lou to think about two problems.

First, the principal needed to react to the letters. Secondly, the superintendent believed that the elementary school needed to study and develop a written policy for assigning students to a classroom. It was agreed that both the principal and the superintendent would consider the problem for a few days and then meet again. There was some urgency, in that members of the Board of Education had been sent copies of several of the letters, and the two administrators knew they would soon be hearing from some of the board members.

## POSSIBLE DISCUSSION QUESTIONS

1. List the alternative methods that might be used to assign students to a teacher in the elementary school. What are the strengths and weaknesses of each approach?

2. What do you feel is the best policy regarding student assignment?

3. What do you think the administration should do about the seven letters?

# Case Study 32

# Authentic Assessment

Perhaps more than any other professionals, educators are constantly experimenting with new methods, as they seek to improve their schools. There are always several innovative concepts or programs featured and educational conferences and school districts themselves frequently bring in consultants to introduce new ideas. Sometimes an "outside expert" makes his or her presentation and there is no follow-up to implement the speaker's ideas, but occasionally a district does become excited enough about an innovation to attempt to implement it in the classroom. When this does occur, there is always a group of teachers who have reservations about the change. Most often, the responsibility for implementing change is left to the principal or those at the department level. It is these middle managers who must deal with the apathy and sometimes the antagonism of the classroom teachers. Even when they are not personally supportive of the new idea, it is their job to carry out district policy.

Bev Jones, social studies coordinator of the Geneva City Schools, was giving high school Principal Dick Stacy a detailed account of her recent meeting with the school's social studies department. It had been a stormy session over a policy statement recently adopted by the District Curriculum Council. After a mandatory three-day workshop for all district faculty, the council, with the strong encouragement of the central administration, had accepted the need to integrate the concept of "authentic assessment" into the academic program. Specifically, they had accepted a new policy which called upon all teachers to develop alternatives to the traditional paper and pencil examination. These new assessment methods were to account for at least 50 percent of all the student grades in the course.

At the workshop, the speaker had argued that the traditional testing procedures were not only an inadequate way to measure a student's knowledge, but they were ineffective in helping teachers judge a student's skill development as well. He was very convincing in making the point that testing should help instructors do a better job teaching and not just allow them to determine a grade.

The second part of the workshop covered the value of student portfolios and other assessment techniques. With the portfolio method, students were required to keep copies of selected work and also maintain a log of their activities in the course. By looking at the portfolio, faculty members could better pinpoint individual learning problems of a student which needed to be addressed. These portfolios could be passed on to the teachers who would work with the students the following year. Teachers in most subject areas were urged to also develop other ways to assess student achievement. Language students could be given oral conversation exercises, while student musicians could be assessed by playing or singing a solo before a panel of music teachers. Both the state and school had accepted learning standards which required students to demonstrate competency in a number of areas, so new assessments had to include components that would measure student competency.

The workshop presenter had been charismatic and effective. His sense of humor and numerous stories had kept the faculty interested for the entire three days, and it was almost impossible to come away from the workshop believing that the teachers were currently doing an adequate job of assessing student progress. It was also true that the speaker had created a good deal of interest among the teachers in the portfolio concept.

The purpose of the department meeting had been to discuss ways to implement the new policy and Bev noted that approximately one-third of the social studies teachers were supportive of the changes. One teacher had said, "Unless we have a policy like this to force us to change, it just won't happen." Another had pointed out that her students already received grades for group projects and making maps and charts. If these projects, along with other essays, were counted, she was already basing close to one-half of her grades on marks for projects other than tests. A third supporter of the policy suggested that the group should look at each of the standards or objectives and talk about alternative ways to assess student progress on each item.

That remark brought to life a second group of social studies teachers who obviously had major reservations about the whole idea of authentic assessment. One veteran teacher suggested that he was still waiting to hear about the research that demonstrated that changing assessment procedures actually improved student achievement. The speaker had talked for three days and mentioned in a favorable light a number of districts that had adopted the idea, but failed to mention any long-term research that clearly validated the change. Bob Pendergrass, the Advanced Placement American History teacher, asked what was wrong with a good test. In his mind at least, the National Advanced Placement History Examination was an excellent way to determine whether the students had learned the subject. The essay questions, he noted, required the students to do much more than just give back objective facts. Someone who did well on these tests probably knew more history than students taking the course at most colleges. In any case, college students would not be judged by their charts, maps, or portfolios, they would be graded on how well they performed on examinations. In fact, their entrance into college would, in large part, depend on how well they did on a standardized test. There were several heads shaking in agreement as Bob made these impassioned remarks, and others expressed their reservations about the portfolio idea. An experienced European history teacher asked, "When am I going to have time in September to read through 120 student portfolios? It is great to say that they will help us to individualize our instruction, but how do we individualize a program for 120 fifteen-year-olds? I think this idea will lower our standards, rather than raise them."

As the meeting had progressed, Bev had also noticed that there was another group of faculty members who remained silent during the discussion. These teachers either did not really care about the new policy or were undecided about whether or not they supported it. In any case, the meeting had ended without the department determining how they would implement the new policy. The Advanced Placement teacher had the last word when he said, "I wish these darn administrators would forget about all of these so-called consultants and just let us do our job!"

As the high school principal listened to the department coordinator, he knew he would have trouble implementing the new policy. Dick had argued against the mandate in the Curriculum Council meeting, but the majority had thought the policy was the only way to ensure that teachers would change. The committee itself included both administrators and classroom teachers, and therefore, the policy was more than an edict from the central office. Still, it was widely understood by the faculty that the hand-picked teachers on the committee tended to be supportive of most curriculum change. More conservative members of the teaching staff seldom found themselves being asked to serve on this powerful committee. When they were appointed, they usually found themselves in the minority.

This was all immaterial, because Dick knew that, along with the social studies coordinator, he would be expected to implement the new policy. He also knew that he was likely to have similar problems with other departments. If the teachers at Geneva High School were going to actually improve their methods for assessing student achievement, the administrators would have to find a way to bring about this change.

## POSSIBLE DISCUSSION QUESTIONS

1. Is the school district attempting to bring about this change in an effective manner? If not, how might the central administration have better approached the implementation process?

2. What, if anything, should a middle manager do when he or she does not support official district policy?

3. What strategy can the district social studies coordinator and the high school principal adopt to help implement this district policy?

## Case Study 33

# It Wasn't a Fair Tryout

When it becomes necessary to make cuts from an athletic team, it is essential that students and parents believe that the system is fair. Being cut can cause a feeling of failure at something our culture admires, and anger is a common reaction if there is a perception that favoritism has been shown in the selection process. To ensure the least possible conflict, schools need to have policies in place that clearly state the criteria being judged. In addition, those making the decision must be seen as being neutral. Any factor which gives credence to possible prejudice in the tryouts can lead to a crisis for a school's administration.

It was not easy to find a cheerleading advisor for the basketball program, as the season ran from November until the end of March. Along with the daily practices, there were twenty or more evening games each year. At least one-half of those games required long bus trips on both weeknights and Friday evenings. As a cheerleading advisor, one was chaperone, coach, personal counselor, and mediator of the frequent squabbles among team members. During his five-year tenure as high school principal, Bob Boyd had helped to hire four different cheerleading advisors. After a year or two on the job, each of these advisors had concluded that it was just too much. This was especially true for the full-time teachers who had served in this capacity. Several had said that their classes were suffering because of the time they were spending on the activity, and one incumbent had calculated her hourly compensation as less than $1.25. She concluded that she "would be better off moonlighting at McDonald's."

The current advisor, Kristen DeHart, was a third-grade teacher in her second year of teaching. Even though her elementary principal had advised her against taking the job, she had decided to try it for a year. Four years experience as a high school cheerleader convinced Kristen that she had the necessary background to help the girls. When Bob and athletic director Stan Seymour interviewed Kristen, they both agreed that she had the right personality for the job. There was no question about her enthusiasm or her knowledge of the activity. She was only twenty-three years old and still had the energy and appearance of a young person. On the other hand, she was mature enough to provide a positive model for the girls on the team. During the interview, she expressed a concern for sportsmanship and discipline, which also seemed appropriate. In addition, Kristen had taken the necessary first aid training which was required for the job. There was also the fact that she was likely to be the only candidate. With two additional vacancies on the coaching staff, the athletic director did not have a lot of time to worry about the cheerleading program, so after a brief orientation, Kristen was ready to choose her squad for the coming season.

There were to be twelve varsity and twelve junior varsity cheerleaders on the squad; the junior varsity team would consist of freshmen and sophomores and the varsity would be made up of juniors and seniors. Several of the members who were trying out had participated on the team last year, and although they would not automatically be chosen, knowing the cheers gave them a great advantage. With over sixty students signed up for the tryouts, selecting the team would be a challenge. To help her, Kristen enlisted three friends who had also been high school cheerleaders to act as judges at the tryouts. There would be three days of practice at which the returning cheerleaders would teach the other candidates three cheers. During the tryouts, the judges would grade the skill level of each of the applicants.

Additionally, Kristen had decided that school citizenship should be a factor in choosing the cheerleaders. She distributed a short questionnaire which asked faculty members to rate students. Although Kristen had mentioned the survey to the athletic director, she had not shown it to either him or the principal before sending it out. The results of the questionnaire would comprise one-third of the students' tryout score and the remaining points would be based on the students' performance of the three cheers.

When the list of the girls who had made the team was posted, all except two of the returning cheerleaders' names appeared. Within two days of posting the tryout results, the athletic director and the principal had received over fifteen calls from parents regarding the selection process, and had been visited by at least that number of students complaining about the tryouts. The objections of the parents and students seemed to center around several issues.

A number of parents believed that the returning cheerleaders had an unfair advantage in that they had done the cheers that were used for the tryouts for over a year. Some other parents had checked into the backgrounds of the three judges and found that one of them had participated in cheerleading for only one year in high school and had not made the high school squad during her senior year. The parent asked how such limited experience qualified her to judge the skill of the candidates.

Although there were other criticisms of the tryouts, the primary source of discontent was the rating scale given to the faculty. This part of the process caused particular criticism, especially after Kristen let it be known that only sixteen of the sixty-two faculty members had bothered to return the questionnaire. Several parents had pointed out to the administration that it was possible these teachers had never taught some of the students they had rated. Others expressed unhappiness with the actual questionnaire which, after the fact, the administration examined and admitted that it might be controversial. Sitting in his office, Bob decided to look at the form again.

Student Name _____

Directions: Using the following scale, note your reaction to the following items.

3—strongly agree    2—agree    1—disagree

1. The student listed above is a good citizen _____.
2. The student listed above works well with others _____.
3. The student listed above will be an excellent role model for other students _____.
4. The student listed above will not be affected adversely in her academic work by participation in the cheerleading squad _____.

Faculty Comments _____
_____
_____

Perhaps the biggest point of contention was whether or not cheerleading was considered a sport. If it was, why should school citizenship even be considered? The basketball players were not rated as school citizens, yet, like the cheerleaders, they represented the school. When parents and students had demanded to see the rating forms and tryout score sheets, Kristen had refused, stating that the information was confidential.

As the controversy became more heated, Bob knew that as principal, he was going to have to react. Even though he was a bit upset with the athletic director for not keeping a more watchful eye on the process, he knew that he himself would ultimately be held responsible. It also seemed that the superintendent and the Board of Education would soon hear of the discontent. In the meantime, Kristen had come to his office in tears and had offered to resign. He assured her that this was not necessary and told her that they would find a way to deal with the problem. The parents were clear on what they wanted. Several of them had made the suggestion that the advisor, parents, and athletic director form a committee to develop a new, more equitable selection process. When a consensus had been reached, a new tryout would be held. This suggestion had become public and Bob had already heard from several of the parents of girls who had been selected for the team. Needless to say, these parents believed that to put everyone through another tryout would be unfair. If a new process was to be developed, they thought that it should be used for the first time next year. In any case, Bob knew that the district would have to think more carefully about how cheerleaders were chosen. Stan, his athletic director, was firmly opposed to a second round of tryouts. He pointed out that after every cut for any team, there were dissatisfied students and parents. To agree to new tryouts would set a terrible precedent. He also argued that it would demonstrate a lack of confidence in the cheerleading advisor. She needed and deserved the support of the administration. Although Stan had made his position clear, Bob knew that he would need to make the final decision.

## POSSIBLE DISCUSSION QUESTIONS

1. Should factors other than cheerleading skill be considered in selecting team members?

2. What do you think the principal should do in this situation?

## Case Study 34

# Bring in the Dogs

There are few schools today that are totally free of drugs and violent student behavior. School boards and administrators have reacted in various ways to these potential problems, and alarmed parents have frequently put pressure on schools to ensure their children's safety. Metal detectors, security guards, drug testing, and locker searches are not uncommon. When a school has a major incident, there are frequently calls for taking drastic action. Administrators must be prepared to deal with such a crisis.

Lakeport had a small high school with approximately 400 students in grades 9 through 12. The district was located in a rural area, although most of the residents worked in a nearby city or its suburbs. Many community members had moved to Lakeport to ensure a safe environment for their children, and had been especially drawn to the fine reputation of its schools. Surrounded by cornfields, the high school campus appeared to be a safe country haven for young people.

Don Katson had been high school principal for twelve years and during that time, there had been a number of fights between students in school. Usually, these had involved two boys fighting over a girl and on rare occasions, it had been two girls engaged in combat. He remembered two or three of these unpleasant skirmishes. Other problems had been caused when a student had said something that was not appreciated by a classmate. Most often, these brief eruptions of violence were broken up quickly and no one had ever been seriously injured. After some mediation in Don's office, he had always been able to get the students to shake hands. The combatants were then suspended until they brought in their parents for a mandatory conference.

Twice during his tenure, marijuana had been discovered in the school building, and on one occasion, a marijuana cigarette had been smoked in the boy's lav. Neither Don nor a deputy from the sheriff's department ever identified the perpetrator. A year ago, on a tip from a student, Don had searched the locker of a boy in the junior class and had found a small quantity of marijuana. The boy was suspended for the remainder of the school year. While this did not seem like an alarming record for a twelve-year period, Don knew that last week's incident went far beyond anything in the past and that it was a matter of concern for the entire school community.

The incident had occurred during the lunch hour when a fight had broken out on the tennis courts outside the school cafeteria. During the spring and fall, students were allowed to go outside after they had eaten lunch, as long as they remained on the tennis court area. One of the two faculty monitors always went outside to chaperone. There were approximately seventy-five students milling around on what was a beautiful spring day. Jane Lindsay, the cafeteria monitor, was talking with several of her English students when she noticed a crowd forming at the far end of the tennis courts. Jane rushed across the court and pushed her way through the crowd where she found two groups of boys glaring menacingly at each other. One group had three boys, the other four. One of the boys had obviously just been punched and had a bloody nose. It was obvious that these two groups were ready to fight and Jane, without hesitating, stepped between them. The boy with the bloody nose glared at her and said angrily, "Mrs. Lindsay, stay out of this!" When she refused to move, he said, "Get out of the way!" He moved toward her and before she knew it, the teacher was in the middle of seven boys punching each other. As she fell to the blacktop, Jane cut her leg and she was unable to extract herself from the melee. At that moment, Coach Faro, a former college football player, pushed his way through the crowd. He bodily picked up one of the students and grabbed another. Bending the boy's arm behind his back, he told him to call off his friends. By the time the coach had the two groups separated, Don and several other faculty members had arrived. One group of boys was ushered to the principal's office, and the other group to the superintendent's office. Before he began to question the boys, Don was handed an open knife that had fallen onto the pavement during the struggle.

After the boys' parents had been called, the principal and the superintendent questioned each of the students. Both sets of boys claimed that the other group had started the fight. The most any of them would say about the cause for the incident was a comment made by a sophomore boy, "Let's just say, Mr. Katson, that we don't like each other." Needless to say, none of the boys had the slightest idea about anything concerning the knife that had been found at the scene of the fight. After the boys were sent home, Don and his assistant principal, Charlene Whitney, spoke with dozens of students who witnessed the fight. According to those few students who were willing to talk, both groups of boys were into drugs. More than one student claimed that their drug use was occurring primarily in a small local mall. There was no evidence that there had been any drugs sold in school or on the school grounds, but as one student said, "These guys have quite a business." The conventional wisdom among the students was that the fight was really between two small drug gangs and was over who was going to control the marijuana trade. As a result of these tips, that Saturday morning, Don, along with a deputy sheriff, came to school and searched the lockers of the accused boys. The search turned up neither drugs nor any additional weapons.

The boys and their parents were summoned to the school for a disciplinary hearing, at which all of the boys disavowed any knowledge of drugs and again claimed to know nothing about the knife that had been found after the fight. Despite the fact that the boys were all prepared to apologize to Mrs. Lindsay for her injury, the superintendent suspended each of them for the remaining seven weeks of the school year. The disciplinary action was taken within days after the incident, but not before the administration had received a letter from the president of the Faculty Association expressing concern about the incident and the injury of one of the groups' members.

Tonight would be the first Board of Education meeting since the incident and Don had heard there was to be a delegation of parents and teachers on hand during the public portion of the meeting and that a number of them were prepared to speak. Over the past week, he had heard numerous suggestions from staff, faculty, students, and parents and expected to hear these recommendations at tonight's meeting. One parent who was concerned about drugs in school had told Don that "it was time to bring in the dogs," referring to the sheriff department's dogs that were trained to identify drugs. Other ideas ranged from hiring security officers for the building to requiring all students to pass through a metal detector upon entering the school. One parent wanted to require drug testing for all students. As these ideas were discussed this evening, there would be a great deal of pressure for the school to take immediate action.

Don couldn't help but think that this was an isolated incident. He wasn't even positive that drugs had been involved in the fight. At the same time, he was beginning to doubt whether he really knew what was going on in his own school and community. In any case, he knew he could not take the incident lightly or appear complacent.

This afternoon, the district administrators would meet to prepare for the Board of Education meeting. As principal, Don knew that along with the superintendent, he would have to give his reaction to the incident. With just a few hours to prepare, he was still not sure of what he should say.

## POSSIBLE DISCUSSION QUESTIONS

1. Are there any additional actions that should have been taken by the administration after the incident?

2. Should the administration make a public statement at the meeting prior to opening the floor for comments? If so, what should they say?

3. Knowing what suggestions are likely to be made during the public portion of the meeting, how should the administration plan to react?

## Case Study 35

# Will You Write a Reference for Me?

Administrators are frequently asked to write recommendations for students, faculty, and staff. Occasionally, such a request can create an ethical and possibly even legal dilemma. This is especially true when the administrator has some reservations about the person making the request. Often, the principal or superintendent might like to be helpful to the individual, but does not wish to mislead a potential employer or college admissions officer. A seemingly simple response is to say to those who can't be endorsed enthusiastically that you prefer not to write a recommendation. Unfortunately, this approach can be complicated, especially when the person has many positive qualities. Another possible solution to difficult requests is to write glowing references for everyone. This method also has its drawbacks, especially when the person recommended turns out to be a flop. Administrators who use this approach run the risk of undermining their own credibility and can lose the respect of their peers.

Two years ago, Karen Little, the elementary principal, had strongly supported the candidacy of Allan Howe for a sixth-grade position. On paper, he was an almost perfect candidate and everyone involved in the hiring decision thought he was a wonderful young man. He had graduated with honors from an excellent teacher education program and had been president of the Future Teachers' Organization. His references from college faculty were exemplary and the supervisor of his practicum had rated him highly. In addition, he had shown great maturity, confidence, and knowledge of educational theory during his interview. Allan's quiet sincerity totally charmed the members of the sixth-grade teaching team, and with the exception of John Lewis, a veteran sixth-grade teacher, everyone involved in the screening and interview supported Allan. John had said, "The young man is just too quiet and academic. I can think of a dozen kids coming through the elementary school who will eat him alive. Sixth graders are not easy these days and this guy is going to have trouble." In the end, John was voted down and the

117

remaining sixth-grade teachers, along with Karen, agreed to send Allan for a final interview with the superintendent.

After two years in the classroom, Karen and the other members of the sixth-grade team now agreed that John Lewis had been right. Everyone had tried to help Allan gain control of his class, but he had just not reached the point where he could maintain sufficient order to provide a viable academic program for his students. During his first year, everyone was hopeful that he was merely experiencing the normal problems of a beginning teacher. Allan was repeatedly advised to be more assertive with several disruptive students whose poor behavior seemed to be contagious. Soon, a majority of the children were frequently ignoring their teacher's instructions. His principal and colleagues visited Allan's class and made numerous suggestions and he was given time to observe other teachers who were successful disciplinarians, but nothing seemed to help. Karen noticed that, at times, the young teacher seemed almost oblivious to the chaos in his classroom. When a student was disrespectful, Allan either ignored the child's comments or tried to reason with the student. While he was talking with one student, others would be acting up. Twice this year, when she had been formally observing his class, Karen had found herself intervening in the lesson to discipline a student.

Even though Allan's first year had been unsuccessful, everyone had hoped that he could improve with a new class in his second year. For two or three weeks that September, it appeared that he was having a better time of it. Unfortunately, by November, conditions in his sixth-grade class were much like the first year. Karen even brought in a classroom management professor from a nearby college to work with Allan, but this, too, seemed to fail. While he was having great difficulty in the classroom, the young teacher remained popular with his fellow faculty members and also developed a good rapport with most of the parents of his students.

For Karen, the decision was a terribly difficult one. She really liked Allan and respected his intellect and sincerity. Even with her fondness for the young teacher, she knew in her heart that he would probably never succeed as a sixth-grade teacher and the input from the members of the sixth-grade team did not alter that judgment. When she discussed the matter with the superintendent, he merely asked, "Have you done everything you can think of to help him?" Karen had answered that, at this point, she could think of nothing else to try. The superintendent's advice had been to say to Allan that things did not seem to be working out in the sixth grade for him, but it was possible that in another district at a different grade level, he would do fine. During her discussion with the young teacher, Karen spoke about his many fine qualities, but told him that she thought it would be best if he resigned at the end of the year. She further recommended that in his resignation letter he cite "personal reasons" for leaving the district. In this way, he could tell others that "he just wanted to do something different."

Allan was not hostile in the meeting, and did not blame the principal for his problems in the classroom; he accepted Karen's advice with grace and good cheer. His fellow teachers felt badly about him leaving and even had a party for him the week after school ended. Even though Karen did not feel good about what she had had to do and had felt awkward when she had encountered Allan during the closing weeks of school, the unfortunate situation seemed to be turning out as well as it could.

On the day after the party for Allan, Karen received a note from him. The short letter thanked her for being a wonderful principal, and in the last paragraph Allan requested that she write a reference for his college placement folder. A copy of the form, which had been included with the letter, asked for a narrative description of the person requesting the recommendation, and did not include a rating scale or objective questions. Although Karen had completed dozens of such forms in the past, she was now in a quandary.

## POSSIBLE DISCUSSION QUESTIONS

1. What are the potential legal problems one should consider when writing a reference?

2. Should the situation with Allan have been handled differently?

3. What would you do if you were the principal in this case?

# Management by E-Mail

Schools, like almost every other organization, have been affected by computers. They have given us considerably more data to help make decisions, and in some situations, do save time. Budgeting and scheduling in most schools are now being done using a computer. It is also likely that more and more schools will soon be in a position to communicate internally by e-mail. Although teachers and principals are behind most large businesses in using electronic communication, it is likely that the computer will soon be found in every classroom. With all of its potential as a teaching tool and a communication device, there still are some problems that can arise.

Tim Davis was sitting reading the newspaper in the corner of the faculty room after having finished his lunch. Even though he was the assistant principal of the elementary school, he still felt at home in the faculty room. He knew that in some schools, administrators stayed away from this teacher haven, but here in the Pembroke Elementary faculty room, he felt quite comfortable. The time spent in the room also helped him to know what the teachers were thinking. They seldom worried about guarding their comments because he was an administrator. Tim hoped this was because they trusted him. He had been the assistant principal for seven years and as the school disciplinarian, he had had occasion to work, at one time or another, with all of the teachers in the building.

As he sat reading his paper, he could not help but overhear the conversation that was taking place at a nearby lunch table. The teachers were talking about the computers that each of them now had in their classrooms. This year, the classrooms had all been wired so that in each room, the teachers had access to the Internet, the library card catalog and the ability to communicate by e-mail. One teacher was talking about how she had begun a correspondence with her six year old grandson in the state of Washington. Another mentioned using the Internet to plan for the family vacation. Eventually, the conversation shifted to how the computer had impacted the school.

One faculty member enthusiastically told how her students had enjoyed doing research on the Internet. In the sixth grade, one classroom was reading about current events from the *Washington Post*, which was available on the Internet. Len Carroll, a veteran sixth grade teacher, made a comment which captured Tim's complete attention. He said, "Do you know what I think the biggest change in the school has been because of our computer network?" He didn't give anyone time to respond, but quickly answered his own question by saying, "What has changed the most is that we now have management by e-mail. Have you noticed that Pat Swanson, our beloved principal, sends us at least two or three e-mail messages every day?" A kindergarten teacher chimed in, "You know, it is true that we rarely see Pat anymore. It used to be that she was frequently in the halls or down in the cafeteria at lunch time. Now, every time I am in the office, her door is closed." A third teacher pointed out that Pat even used to come into the faculty room occasionally. "I'll tell you what happened," Len said. "Our principal has become a computer nerd."

He went on to discuss a recent conversation he had had with the two secretaries in the principal's office. They had shared with him "confidentially" that Pat now did most of her own typing and was keeping most of her files on the computer. The secretaries' role in the office had become almost solely to answer the telephone and act as receptionists. One of the secretaries had confided that when Pat's door was closed, they had found themselves trying to solve some of the problems the principal normally would have dealt with herself. Often, she reported, the secretaries would go for hours without seeing or talking to their boss. When Pat closed her door, it was a signal that she was not to be bothered.

Ruth Jordan, a special education teacher, asked, "What could she possibly be doing with the computer, except sending us memos? That doesn't take very long." Len reported that the secretaries had said that Pat was spending a considerable amount of time making spreadsheets for reports to the central office. Betty Lansing, the principal's primary secretary, told Len that she thought that Pat had really changed and she felt that her role as a school secretary has been diminished. Ruth went on to say, "I really feel sorry for the girls in the office, but the problem is bigger than that. Pat used to be a people person, and now she seems to have become a computer person. Someone should talk to her." A young kindergarten teacher who had been listening to the conversation commented, "Sure, I will waltz right into her office and tell her, 'Pat, baby, you'd better shape up!'"

On hearing all of this, Tim was not completely surprised. He knew that during her eleven year career, Pat had developed a reputation as being a competent, nononsense administrator. Although she was not personally close with any of the faculty, she had earned their respect. At the same time, she was perceived by some as being slightly remote and possibly oversensitive. It was unlikely that any of the teachers or the secretaries would feel comfortable talking with her about how she was being perceived.

Unlike other employees of the school, Tim had developed a somewhat closer relationship with his boss. At least until this year, he had spent a good deal of time in her office, where they were able to talk freely about the problems facing the school. Although they were not close outside of school, in her office, Pat seemed quite at ease with her assistant principal. Both of them knew that their skills and personalities complemented each other. Tim had always thought that they were a good team. Still, they were not what he would consider friends.

In the years they had worked together, he had disagreed with Pat a number of times, but he had never said anything that she could construe as criticism. He remembered vividly an occasion several years ago when the superintendent had written her a note suggesting that she might do something differently in the future. Pat was livid and talked about little else for at least a week. Perhaps, Tim reflected, she wasn't as secure and confident as she appeared to be on the surface. In any case, he did not look forward to talking with her about the conversation he had just overheard. Still, he knew that if anyone was going to raise the issue with Pat, it was probably going to be him. He thought briefly about talking with Steve Crowe, the assistant superintendent, but that did not seem fair to Pat. There was no question that Tim would have to talk to her himself.


## POSSIBLE DISCUSSION QUESTIONS

1. Is it an administrator's role to communicate this type of criticism to his or her supervisor in the organization?

2. What should Tim say to Pat?

3. Should a building principal spend time during the school day working on a computer?

## Case Study 37

# The Sit-In

Occasionally, administrators are forced to deal with students who engage in civil disobedience. Although it may only happen once or twice during a principal's career, such an incident will undoubtedly be one that will be talked about in the community. The media will be interested and there may even be a television camera crew to deal with. While schools try to develop policies to guide administrators in most situations, it is unlikely that there will be a page in the policy manual that refers to student demonstrations. The Board of Education and the public judge a district administrator or a principal by how well they react during such a crisis. If the administrator has developed a level of trust and respect with the student leaders, there will be a much better chance of successfully dealing with a student uprising. In this case study, the administrator is new to the school and does not have such an advantage.

The Roosevelt High School School for the Arts was one of the two or three most popular magnet schools in the city. Each year, hundreds of students either auditioned or presented art portfolios in the hope of being selected. Of the approximately 600 who had applied last year, only 200 were accepted. In years past, there had been a quota system that ensured that the number of African-American, Hispanic, and Caucasian students accepted would be based on the percentages of each group in the community, and although this policy had been abolished two years ago, the makeup of the student body remained a controversial issue in the city. Still, the school was one of the most fully integrated in the district and for the most part, students got along quite well. This was aided by the fact that the numerous performing groups and athletic teams were thoroughly integrated, and there was also some interracial student dating.

Nonetheless, there had always been fairly clear divisions, for example in the school cafeteria. Most of the African-Americans sat in their own area, as did the Hispanics and Caucasians. The only significantly mixed group was the football team and the cheerleading squad, who had taken a long table in the middle of the room.

Laura, who had been principal for three months, was very worried about the lack of integration in the student body. She had made it one of her personal objectives for the year to try to find ways to bring the student body together. Unfortunately, her first weeks on the job had been so hectic that she had not time to think about this goal and had yet to come up with a plan to address the problem. Still, the school year was off to a good start. The football team had already won three games, which had made this the most successful season in school history. There had been no serious discipline problems and the two fall concerts had received standing ovations from appreciative audiences. The first art show of the year was currently in progress and parents were turning out in large numbers to admire their children's work.

Perhaps she had fallen into a state of complacency, because Laura was totally caught off guard when the trouble began over the tryouts for the school musical, one of the major presentations of the school year. The school went all out for these musical comedies that had had sell out crowds for the past four years, and they provided a showcase for the special talents of the student body. The art students created elaborate sets, the orchestra in the pit was always outstanding, and the leads and the chorus were chosen from a pool of exceptionally talented students. There was no greater honor during the school year than to be selected for a major part in the musical, and because so many students auditioned, the tryouts lasted for three weeks.

After the leads for the show had been posted, there was great jubilation by a few and tears of disappointment by many. Over the next three days, students and parents analyzed who had been chosen for the leads, and it was soon noted that none of the seven major roles in the play were assigned to Caucasian students. This surprised everyone, given the fact that the musical's faculty advisors were white, along with the vast majority of the faculty. The student body itself was 45 percent Afro-American, 35 percent Hispanic, and 25 percent Caucasian. Two of the disappointed Caucasian female students had come to see Laura, claiming that the selection of leads was an example of reverse discrimination. One of the girls, Student Council Vice President Jennifer Lowe, told Laura that, as a vocalist, she had received a 6A rating at a solo competition last spring. This was the highest grade possible and had been on the most difficult music available for presentation. She also noted that she had done well in a major part in the musical in her junior year, as well as participating in summer theater work. There was no question that she had more stage experience than those students chosen for the female leads in the musical.

Laura attempted to explain to the girls that they were wrong in thinking that the selection had anything to do with affirmative action. Both girls argued that the district was trying to keep whites in the public schools and that the School for the Arts had the highest concentration of whites among the city schools. Jennifer was quite clear that she believed that "if you don't treat the whites fairly, they are not going to want to be here." The girls also mentioned that their parents agreed with them on this issue and in fact, the majority of the white students and their parents were very upset. Laura said that she understood their disappointment, but that there was no question in her mind that the tryouts had been fair. When the girls left her office, the principal knew that she had not convinced them that they had not been discriminated against by the school.

Even knowing this, Laura was not prepared for what happened next. Following the final lunch period that day, approximately one hundred white students walked out of the building and sat down quietly around the flagpole. As she looked out her window, Laura could see Jennifer addressing the group. Pulling up the driveway was a van that had the WKYP-TV logo on its side, and she also recognized the education reporter from the city's only newspaper talking to one of the students. Obviously, Laura was the last person to have heard about the upcoming protest and she wondered how this had been kept a secret. It seemed unlikely that a faculty member had not picked up a hint that there was to be a demonstration. As she continued to look out her window, Laura saw a television cameraman take his camera out of the van. Laura had a sinking feeling in her stomach, but she knew that she had to act.

## POSSIBLE DISCUSSION QUESTIONS

1. Could the principal have done more to head off the protest?

2. Now that the sit-in has begun, what should Laura do?

# Case Study 38

# The Gun

A recent number of incidents involving students bringing and using guns in school have highlighted this problem nationwide. On May 25, 1998, the *Washington Post* published the results of a poll showing that an estimated one million students had seen another student with a gun in school. A total of three million students who responded to the poll said that they "personally knew someone who had brought a gun to school in the previous six months." In certain high crime districts, as many as one-half of the students personally knew someone who had carried a gun to school. Although many of the students having this experience attend urban schools, there have been enough examples of problems in rural and suburban schools to know that guns can be found anywhere. The societal problems that have created this phenomenon are many and varied, but whatever the reasons, school administrators must be prepared to do what is necessary to attempt to prevent violence in their schools.

Despite the tragic stories in the national press and on television, few people ever expected a student to bring a gun into the Pinehurst Middle School, but it had happened. Fortunately, the gun was not used and the incident was dealt with without any personal injury or interruption of the school day. Still, the events of last Thursday were very clear in Principal Ron Clark's mind.

He had been sitting in his office eating a ham sandwich he had brought from home that day when Mrs. Pringle, his secretary, rang him to say that Mary Lake, a seventh-grade student, wished to see him. She had told the secretary that "it was an emergency." Ron invited Mary into his office, asked her to have a seat, and attempted to put the very nervous student at ease. It was obvious, however, that Mary was not there for small talk. She quickly blurted out that "David Lease has a gun in school!" Ron asked if she had seen it herself, and she responded impatiently, "No, but Rachel saw it." Ron called Mrs. Pringle and asked her to have Rachel Nottingham come to his office. His impression was that Rachel was something of a "busybody," and he recalled that she had even angered some fellow students by spreading rumors. Yet even though he questioned her credibility, he knew that it was necessary to talk to the girl.

Rachel was unequivocal in her insistence that she had seen David showing Brian Kelley the gun in the hall. "Are you sure it was a real gun?" Ron asked. Indignant, Rachel had responded, "I know a pistol when I see one. My Dad has one and I know this one was real!" Ron asked the girl why she had not reported what she had seen. Rachel admitted that the last thing she had wanted to do was to make David mad at her.

After thanking the girls and sending them back to class, the principal decided that Rachel's report was enough to justify a search of David's locker. Looking through the locker and its contents carefully, Ron found nothing. At this point, it occurred to him that before he did anything else, he should call the local police. Still, he was not totally convinced that there was really any danger and just the presence of the police in the building could be disruptive. After checking David's schedule, he walked down to the seventh-grade science classroom. Looking in the door's window, he caught the teacher's attention. She came to the door and Ron asked if she would have David come into the hall. When David joined him, the principal asked the boy if he had brought a gun to school. Pausing for a split second, David denied having a gun and asked the principal, "Do you want to search me?" Ron said, "If you don't mind, I guess I will." A quick search of the thirteen-year-old's pockets did not yield a gun and Ron told the boy that he was sorry to have bothered him.

Just as he was about to allow David to return to class, it occurred to him that the boy might have a book bag in the classroom. Leaving David sitting in the hall, Ron entered the room and asked Mrs. Stevens where David had been sitting. There was a blue knapsack under the chair. Quickly unzipping the bag, Ron put his hand in and found a small pistol. Momentarily shocked, he left the gun in the bag, put it under his arm and went to join David in the hall. When he stepped into the hall, however, the boy was gone.

It was late that evening when the police found David sleeping on a park bench. Within a week, the boy was given a formal hearing and was suspended from school for the remainder of the year. The school district sent tutors to his home to ensure that he could complete the seventh-grade work. Ron recalled that during the hearing, David had claimed that he had no plan to use the gun. It had not been loaded and he did not have ammunition with him in school. David's reason for bringing the gun had been to scare off some other kids who had been "hassling him in school." He had thought that if the other students knew that he had a gun, they would leave him alone.

Stories about the gun spread rapidly in the community and most of the rumors made the situation much worse than it really was. Alarmed parents called the school and asked what was going to be done to ensure their childrens' safety, and the issue came up at the middle school Parent Teacher Association meeting. Ron had assured the parents that the administration was considering several options and that a report would be given at the next Board of Education meeting. Having said that, Ron knew he was ensuring an audience at the next board meeting. As a result of a conversation with the superintendent, Ron was asked to find out what other schools in the area were doing about the potential danger of guns in school. He learned that in the city's secondary schools, security guards were assigned throughout the building, and several of the schools used metal detectors to screen everyone entering the building. A number of assembly programs stressing the danger of firearms and the futility of violence were also available to schools.

Other than these rather conventional ideas, Ron had come up with nothing. He knew that if the administration merely placed the blame on society's problems, parents would not be satisfied. Comments that were critical of gun owners would also not be well received by some parents. While he didn't know exactly what to do, Ron was now sure that a tragedy like the ones he had read about in the newspaper could very well happen at Pinehurst Middle School.

## POSSIBLE DISCUSSION QUESTIONS

1. What, if anything, would you have done differently upon hearing that there was a gun in school?

2. If you were Ron, what would you recommend at the upcoming Board of Education meeting?

*Case Study 39*

# There's Just Too Much Paperwork!

Whether large or small, schools are bureaucracies, and as all administrators in our society, school managers spend significant amounts of time with paperwork. The hours spent completing reports, processing requisitions, and writing grants often rob the school administrator of opportunities to personally interact with students, faculty, and parents. Although steps can be taken to minimize paperwork within a district, some of it is generated outside the school district. While there is no way to completely eliminate this aspect of a school administrator's duties, systems that keep paperwork to a minimum can be devised. This is a legitimate goal, because school administration should be primarily a "people business."

After almost a year as a school principal in a large city high school, John Sanders was not really happy in his job. Having spent five years as a principal in a smaller school, his duties this year had been very different than he had expected. While John had had no assistant principals in his previous position, he still seemed to have time to interact with students and faculty. He had done all of the classroom observations, dealt with discipline, and offered in a number of curriculum initiatives.

Even though he now had three assistant principals, he had little time for any of these activities. It did not take a great deal of analysis on John's part to determine why he was having a problem. Two factors quickly came to mind. First, he was spending a great deal of time on paperwork. In addition to the required weekly and monthly reports for the central office, he had to compile weekly the discipline records of his three assistants plus do a comprehensive report that included every discipline incident they had dealt with that week. This included not just the numbers, but often a detailed explanation for certain types of problems as well.

John was handling all of the budget requisitions of the faculty and staff. In his first month on the job, it had become clear that he would frequently be asked by the central office to justify expenditures. In preparation for these questions, John took the time to confer with those requesting budgeted funds. Preparing and coordinating budget requests for the coming year had taken a considerable amount of his time. There were also periodic reports to the central office on faculty and staff evaluations, and even though these were being done by his assistants, he was responsible for reading and signing each evaluation. The assistant superintendent for personnel was frequently on the phone quizzing him on whether certain employees were effective in their jobs.

John was shocked when he learned that it was also part of the principal's job to develop the master schedule. In his previous school, a guidance counselor had been responsible for the schedule. Even with a computer, he found that he spent hours working with the department chairs to put together the amazingly complicated puzzle. For weeks at a time, he had closed his door and spent most of his day developing the budget, devising the master schedule, and dealing with emergencies.

There was another problem that had become increasingly obvious during the year. Even though he had worked as an assistant principal in the district for five years, Ron Claus came to John almost every day for advice on how to deal with student and faculty problems. It seemed that whenever there was the possibility of any conflict, Ron would seek the principal's input. John knew that he had spent twice as much time with Ron during the past year than he had with the other two assistant principals combined.

This past year, many of his working hours had been spent on writing the computer grant. The school district no longer had a grant writer on staff and building principals who wanted to bring federal or state money into their schools were encouraged to prepare their own grants. His predecessor, Louise Harris, had been awarded $50,000 to establish a computer lab, and although the original funding on that grant had run out, it was possible to apply for an extension. John had felt that he needed to at least try for the extra money, but never having prepared a grant in the past, he had not realized the amount of time it would take. As he thought about the year that was about to end, John concluded that the organizational pattern of his school caused almost all of the required paperwork to be done by the principal. His predecessor had purposely organized the school in that way as she had disliked handling the day-to-day discipline work and had not really been interested in doing classroom visitations. Her primary interests apparently had been in financial management and had written her dissertation on how schools could be managed more like businesses. In fact, this interest in educational finance had been instrumental in helping her to be appointed an assistant superintendent for business in another district. John knew that his favorite part of the job was not working with budgets, schedules, or grants. He was sure that he could make a contribution if he had the time to mentor teachers, work with students, and help with curriculum change. Also, he knew that he should not spend nearly so much time giving advice to Ron Claus.

There was no question that he would be happier and more effective as a building principal if he could change the organizational pattern of his school. Currently, each of the three assistant principals was assigned to one of the three grade levels in the building, and each was in charge of discipline for that level. The faculty was divided so that each assistant was assigned three departments and the chairs of each department reported directly to their assistant principal. Together with the department chairs, the assistant principals would do the required classroom observations and annual evaluations. The only classroom visitations that John had made during the year had been five observations of teachers who had been eligible for tenure. He was still having trouble remembering the names of some of the teachers in the school and most of the 105 faculty members had not even been in his office during his first year on the job. As principal, his primary interaction with the teaching staff had been during the monthly faculty meetings and his work with department chairs on budgets and scheduling.

With the exception of the department chairs, he had not really become well acquainted with any of the teachers, and the only staff members he had gotten to know were his secretary and the head of maintenance. John had spent a good deal of time with the three assistant superintendents at the central office and had attended frequent meetings with his fellow principals and the superintendents. He knew that he would always be spending time in the central office, but it was possible that changes could be made within his school. After graduation, reorganization was going to be his first priority.

## POSSIBLE DISCUSSION QUESTIONS

1. What should John do about the frequency of Ron's visits to his office?

2. Is there a best way to organize the administrative work in a large school? If so, how would you do it?

3. If you were John, what organizational pattern would you devise?

4. Given the same size school, (2,000 students, 105 faculty, and 3 assistant principals) how would you organize the duties if you were the high school principal?

## Case Study 40

# I Just Wanted to Do Something Useful

Increasingly, schools are recognizing the value of using volunteer help. These individuals can relieve and assist the professional staff with numerous tasks such as making photocopies, shelving books, and tutoring. Some of the helpers are young parents, but others are senior citizens looking for ways to help children, some volunteers may have college degrees, while others may be high school dropouts. Nearly all of those who offer their services want to be helpful and volunteers bring to the school not only diverse backgrounds, but a great variety of skills. The challenge for the school administrator is to find an appropriate role for each volunteer. In this way, they can be a positive addition to a school. If the district lacks a plan, on the other hand, problems are likely to arise.

Sandy Crosby was the first person to hold the title of assistant principal at the Belva Lockwood Elementary School. The 720-student body had become too much for one administrator. Grace Northrup, the principal, had requested that the school board give her an assistant three years ago and it had taken that long to convince a majority of the Board of Education. Once it was authorized, the board members themselves had taken an active part in the selection process.

Sandy had been chosen by the board and the administration after a long screening process. Only twenty-eight years old, she had impressed everyone with her enthusiasm and high energy level. More than any of the other candidates, she seemed to have a number of creative ideas for improving the school. One idea that particularly appealed to both Grace and the board members was Sandy's concept of a volunteer program. Especially attractive was the notion of recruiting senior citizens to help out. One of the board members observed at Sandy's interview that "having the old folks in the school might get some of them to vote for the budget."

As the school year began, Sandy and Grace agreed that one of Sandy's goals for the coming year was the establishment of a volunteer program for the school.

Sandy decided on two strategies to recruit the volunteers. First, she submitted to the superintendent an article for the monthly school newsletter urging people to volunteer. The article outlined some of the possible jobs volunteers might perform and asked that interested individuals call Sandy at the elementary school. Her second recruitment plan was to speak at a luncheon at the senior citizens' center.

Sandy knew that she should also begin to talk to the faculty and asked Grace for five minutes at the October meeting to talk about the volunteer program. During that time, Sandy requested that all teachers who would like to be involved with the first volunteers stop by her office to discuss the types of help they could use. Sandy's first surprise in setting up the program was a letter that she received two days after the faculty meeting. The executive committee of the teachers' union wrote that, although they supported the idea of volunteers, the membership would become concerned if volunteers were given "professional duties to perform." The letter went on to say, "Volunteers should never be used as a rationale for increasing class size. We wish to make it known that, given a choice, the faculty would prefer well-trained, paid teacher aides who would be in the classroom every day and not merely there on a 'hit or miss' schedule." At first, Sandy was quite miffed with the letter, but together with Grace, a response was prepared. Their reply assured the union that there was no intention to use volunteers as a way to reduce the teaching staff or to increase class size and offered to work with the union to develop a mutually agreed upon volunteer program. Several weeks had passed and the union had not responded to the letter.

Sandy was also disappointed with the number of faculty members who came forward to participate in the program. The first to volunteer was the school librarian, who wanted people to shelve books and update the card catalog. The school secretaries also requested help in making photocopies and filing. Only four teachers talked to Sandy and they were primarily interested in having someone make photocopies and help with bulletin boards.

The response from the school newsletter and her visit with the senior citizens was less than encouraging. She had garnered only seven volunteers, three senior citizens and four parents. Meeting with each of them separately, she attempted to determine the kind of work they would like to do. The volunteers ranged from a unmarried teenage mother to a seventy-five-year-old retired teacher. Six of the seven said that they really wanted to work with children in the classroom and one only wanted to work in her son's room to help him get better grades. From the interviews, Sandy could see that the volunteers pictured themselves as assistant teachers who would be tutoring or reading to the children. Sandy was worried that the volunteers might feel that shelving books or standing for hours at a photocopy machine was not really what they had in mind, yet she had no alternative but to try to match the volunteers with the faculty and staff who had agreed to participate. Each of the volunteers was given a job and Sandy decided to observe the results before trying to expand the program.

It was only a few weeks until problems began to arise. The first volunteer to work with Sandy had earned a degree in teacher education fourteen years earlier. Although the woman had never actually taught, she had some strong ideas about what should go on in a third-grade classroom. She told Sandy that in Miss Langdon's class "there was just too much freedom and students were wandering around all of the time." She was also concerned that Miss Langdon never used the language arts workbooks or the spelling books, saying, "She is into this whole language stuff and I am not sure that these students are really learning to read."

Sandy had not really thought about the possibility that some volunteers might be critical of what was going on in the classrooms. The program was supposed to help public relations, not create new critics. The retired teacher was appalled by the noise level in the library and the cafeteria and also disapproved of the way students moved about in the halls. She told Sandy, "In my day, children were taught to act like ladies and gentlemen and when they didn't, somebody spanked their behinds." The volunteer also commented that her husband had questioned why the school was spending so much on computers for the classrooms. As he put it, "Those machines are not going to teach anyone to read or do arithmetic. Why do we need them in the first-grade classroom?"

Another parent volunteer came in to complain about the menial task she was being given to perform. She pointed out that she was a college graduate and all she was doing was working at the photocopying machine and shelving books. "I just wanted to do something useful," she told Sandy, "I think I have more to offer than being just a glorified clerk."

Even several of the teachers complained about the program. A sixth-grade teacher noted that his volunteer was much too eager to give unsolicited advice, and another commented on the irregular attendance of her helper. The teacher would prepare several tasks, but at the last minute the volunteer would call the school office and leave a message that something had come up and that she wouldn't be in that day.

After just two months, Sandy knew that her volunteer program was off to a less than successful beginning. It was evident to her that before she attempted to expand it, she needed to reevaluate what had happened so far. As a new administrator, Sandy was determined that her first major program not turn out to be a failure.

## POSSIBLE DISCUSSION QUESTIONS

1. What might Sandy have done differently in launching her volunteer program?

2. List the essential aspects of a successful school volunteer program.

3. What can Sandy do to improve her current situation?

# About the Author

Bill Hayes has been a high school social studies teacher, department chairman, assistant principal, and a high school principal. From 1973 to 1994, he served as superintendent of schools for the Byron-Bergen Central School District, which is located eighteen miles west of Rochester, New York. During his career, he was an active member of the New York State Council of School Superintendents and is the author of a Council publication entitled *The Superintendency: Thoughts for New Superintendents*, which is used to prepare new superintendents in New York State. Mr. Hayes has also written a number of articles for various educational journals. Since his retirement in 1994, he has chaired the Teacher Education Division at Roberts Wesleyan College in Rochester, New York. As a companion to this book, Mr. Hayes has also written *Real-Life Case Studies for Teachers*, available from Scarecrow Press.